Cryptocurrency for Next-Gen Wealth

Understand the Core Concepts of Crypto & DeFi to Envision the Future of Finance Beyond Just Bitcoin, Invest Smart with Clarity & Confidence

Troy Brexton

A Quick Gift for Readers

Before You Begin

Thank you for picking up this book—I'm truly glad you're here.

If you'd like to go deeper, I regularly share **bonus chapters, exclusive content, and early previews** through my BookFunnel VIP list. It's a simple way to get even more value from what you've already started here.

Claim your free bonus here:

https://dl.bookfunnel.com/w30ai1rzn6

Let's keep learning, growing, and thriving—together.

Contents

Introduction

Many years ago, I attended a tech conference where a speaker passionately spoke about Bitcoin. He explained that even though it was new at the time, it could eventually grow into something big—he used the words "revolutionize money." It seemed as if he thought cryptocurrency's potential was infinite.

At first, I was skeptical. I had a hard time believing that people would move their life savings out of banks and into something risky like crypto wallets. I didn't doubt that it would get institutional interest, but I never expected Bitcoin to become a popular investment for ordinary people. And the concept of it being exchanged as seamlessly as the U.S. dollar felt far-fetched. Never in my wildest dreams would I have imagined a country would adopt it as legal tender the way El Salvador did in 2021 (Kolakowski, 2021).

However, the more I learned, the more I realized Bitcoin was different than anything that had come before. The blockchain that it ran on was truly revolutionary. It wasn't just about having money on your computer. It was far more than that. This knowledge ignited a passion in me to explore and understand even more about cryptocurrency.

Nowadays, crypto is no longer a niche interest or a passing trend. It's a force reshaping modern finance. With Bitcoin's market cap surpassing $1 trillion and decentralized finance (DeFi) platforms gaining traction, cryptocurrency is attracting attention from the government, big financial institutions, and everyday investors. Cryptocurrencies like Ethereum have emerged alongside Bitcoin as key pillars in this new ecosystem. The rise of non-fungible tokens (NFTs) has captured headlines, bringing digital assets to the forefront of pop culture. Celebrities from all walks of life have created their own NFTs, from rapper Snoop Dogg to actress Lindsey Lohan and even *Monty Python* creator John Cleese (Dedezade, 2021).

This book is designed to offer you a straightforward introduction to cryptocurrency (or crypto, for short). The goal is to demystify complex concepts and provide insights into crypto's big philosophical questions. Whether you are a beginner, a tech-savvy investor, or someone skeptical about crypto's legitimacy, the aim is to empower you with clarity and confidence.

In the following chapters, we'll talk about several key subjects related to crypto.

1. You'll gain foundational knowledge about what cryptocurrencies are and how they function.
2. We'll delve into investment strategies and discuss the potential for maximizing returns. This includes looking at the philosophical aspects of decentralization, transparency, and democratization.
3. You'll learn about blockchain technology, the backbone of all cryptocurrencies.

There are a lot of myths and misconceptions out there about crypto. Some people view it as a tool only for illicit activities. Others think it's too volatile or complex for the average person to understand and use. The truth is that these myths come from somewhere, but they don't tell the whole story. This book is a balanced view of crypto backed by credible information. That way, you can make your own judgments based on the facts. Whether you're someone new to crypto without much knowledge or someone tech-savvy who has been engaged with it for years, my hope is that you'll find value here.

The following chapters will also include a plethora of real-world examples, historical context, and technical details to enrich your understanding. We'll start by looking at the history of cryptocurrency, which began way back in 2009 when a mysterious figure calling themselves Satoshi Nakamoto introduced Bitcoin to the world. Back then, Bitcoin was hardly worth anything. In 2010, a Florida man named Laszlo Hanyecz purchased two pizzas from Papa John's for 10,000 Bitcoins. Today, those Bitcoins would be worth almost a billion dollars (Coinbase, n.d.-c).

Since then, the crypto ecosystem has evolved rapidly. New coins like Ethereum, Solana, and Chainlink have gained traction, offering solutions to make crypto faster and more secure. Stablecoins have given people methods for protecting their assets from the volatility in Bitcoin, Ethereum, and other coins. Memecoins have drawn in new investors, finding a place among coins like Ethereum and Cardano that have real use cases. These are just some of the things we'll discuss as we move through these pages.

By the time you finish, you will have the knowledge and confidence to navigate crypto. Whether your goal is to invest, increase your awareness, or just learn something new, you'll be better equipped.

So, let's go ahead and dive in. Together, we'll uncover crypto's mysteries and broaden your understanding of how it shapes our present and might shape the future.

Chapter 1
Laying the Groundwork

If you're like me, you might be asking yourself, "Can digital money truly rival traditional currency?" That's a fair question. Since that day back in 2010 when Bitcoin was used to purchase pizza, it hasn't exactly gained much traction as a currency for buying everyday goods. As of 2025, most people exchanging crypto are still doing so for investment reasons. That said, it's still come a long way.

Back in 2010, crypto was nothing more than an experiment. There was no telling if it would last or not. Virtual currencies had come and gone before. For instance, eCash was created in 1990 by David Chaum but it went defunct by 1998 (Redman, 2024). Bitcoin is different, and not just because it's lasted more than twice as long. The virtual currencies of this era, which thrive because they are decentralized, have achieved adoption on a previously unprecedented scale.

As you'll see in the following chapters, crypto now stands at the forefront of economic transformations. Bitcoin has been bought by large financial institutions such as BlackRock and big-name public figures like Mark Cuban and Jack Dorsey (Meiterman, 2025). El Salvador adopted Bitcoin as a legal tender. When Russia declared war on Ukraine, there were calls by Ukrainian nonprofits for donations in cryptocurrency, which was one of the fastest ways for them to raise money. Multiple Bitcoin Exchange Traded Funds (ETFs) are now traded on the stock exchange, as is Coinbase, a public company that specializes in all things crypto.

As a result, crypto is reshaping how we think about value, transactions, and financial systems. Understanding cryptocurrency's complex nature begins with grasping its roots as a digital asset—a concept that challenges conventional notions of money and decentralization.

Demystifying Cryptocurrency: A Beginner's Guide

Cryptocurrency is a digital or virtual currency that uses cryptography for security. Unlike traditional currencies issued by governments, cryptocurrencies operate on a technology called blockchain, ensuring transparency and immutability. Bitcoin, the first and most well-known cryptocurrency, has now been joined by thousands of others, including Ethereum, which has been the second biggest one for many years now. While traditional currencies rely on central banks and physical forms, cryptocurrencies exist purely in electronic form. A key feature is that they are decentralized, meaning that no one person or entity is required to keep the network running. This decentralization is also a philosophical shift, emphasizing user control and reducing reliance on one centralized authority like a bank or a government.

Cryptocurrencies were created to address specific flaws in the current financial system. For instance, one notable goal is financial inclusivity. By removing traditional barriers*, cryptocurrencies provide access to financial services for unbanked populations globally. Additionally, they aim to reduce transaction costs and times. Traditional money transfers can take days and incur high fees, especially across borders. Cryptocurrencies offer near-instantaneous transactions with minimal fees, making them attractive for both individuals and businesses seeking efficiency.

***Traditional Barriers in the Financial System**

Traditional barriers in the financial system include requirements such as bank accounts, credit histories, and physical access to banking institutions, which exclude millions of individuals worldwide. A recent World Bank study revealed that there are currently 1.7 billion unbanked people across the globe. That's about 25% of Earth's population (Bertch, 2024)! Additionally, high fees and slow processing times, particularly for cross-border transactions, further limit accessibility and efficiency, leaving many without essential financial services.

At the heart of any cryptocurrency transaction are public and private keys. Imagine you have a PO Box or a mailbox from which you can receive or send mail. Your public key is like your mailbox's address

—anyone can use it to send money to you. Your private key is like the key that the post office gives to you for your PO Box or the key that you use to open your mailbox—it's only available to you, allowing you to access and spend the money inside. When you make a transaction, it gets recorded on the blockchain, which is a decentralized ledger akin to the records of your mailing history a post office might keep. Each transaction entry includes a timestamp, the sender's pseudonymous address, the recipient's address, and the amount sent. This makes the blockchain fully transparent. For example, if you send Bitcoin to a friend, everyone can see that a transaction happened and how much was sent, but your personal identity remains private because transactions are linked to pseudonymous codes, not real names. This combination of openness and privacy is why cryptocurrencies are so trusted and appealing.

That said, there are some misconceptions. For example, many people think that crypto provides complete anonymity, making it a tool for illegal activities. In reality, transactions are pseudonymous, which means they use unique addresses instead of names, but can still be traced on the transparent blockchain—often helping law enforcement track illicit activity. Another common belief is that cryptocurrencies are always volatile and speculative. While prices can fluctuate, this is influenced by factors like market demand, adoption, and regulatory news in a way similar to other financial markets. Fluctuations in the cryptocurrency market are a bit more pronounced because crypto is still young.

Blockchain 101: The Backbone of Digital Currencies

Cryptocurrencies can be transacted in a decentralized way thanks to something called the blockchain. This is a decentralized ledger system that records transactions across multiple computers, aka a distributed network*. This ensures that the data in the ledger is secure and transparent, making it less vulnerable to manipulation and fraud.

Here's how the blockchain works:

- An element known as a block contains a set of transactions.
- These blocks are linked together in a chronological chain.

- Blocks can't be changed since the data is stored on many computers, and they must all match up for the data to be valid. Once data is entered into the blockchain, it's there forever.
- Transactions or changes need to be approved before they are added to the blockchain. This can be done in a variety of different ways, and the exact method depends on the process defined by the individual blockchain, such as the Bitcoin blockchain or the Ethereum blockchain.
- Blockchains can also be used in non-financial contexts, such as for keeping records of medical information (Hayes, 2024).

*Distributed Network

A distributed network in blockchain is a system where data is stored across multiple computers or nodes instead of a central server. Each node holds a copy of the blockchain and works together to validate transactions. This decentralized structure enhances security, transparency, and reliability, as no single point of failure or control exists within the network.

The process of validating and recording transactions on the blockchain involves a method known as mining. This is where computers on the network, called nodes, use computational power to solve complex mathematical problems. Once solved, these problems validate the authenticity of transactions, allowing them to be added to the blockchain. However, before this can happen, all nodes must agree on the validity of the transaction. This helps to maintain the integrity of the blockchain. This is also called the consensus mechanism. If you ever send Bitcoin or another cryptocurrency, you can track this process and see it happening in real time. Sites like Blockstream will show you how many confirmations a transaction has.

The most common consensus mechanism protocol is proof-of-work (PoW). It's used by Bitcoin and, until recently, it was used for most other cryptocurrencies. However, new methods like proof-of-stake are emerging, offering more energy-efficient alternatives (proof-of-work and proof-of-stake (PoS) will be explained in more detail later).

The key to all of this is the distributed ledger system, which records transactions across many nodes, ensuring data redundancy and resilience. This prevents any single entity from having control over the entire network, thus making the network secure and trustworthy.

Beyond cryptocurrency, the blockchain has many uses. In the broader world of finance, it can facilitate instant transaction settlements, bypassing traditional intermediaries like banks. For example, cross-border payments using blockchain platforms like Ripple can be completed in seconds rather than days.

In healthcare, the blockchain can be used to securely manage patient data. Healthcare providers can use decentralized electronic health records (EHRs) to create a permanent, accessible record of each patient's medical history, which improves communication between healthcare providers and the accuracy of information. Similarly, it can also be used to record information on healthcare providers, keeping track of credentials, certifications, and licenses to more easily manage verification processes (Thompsett, 2024).

In the supply chain, companies like Maersk and Fr8 are already using the blockchain to make processes more efficient and secure. Maersk uses a private blockchain network to track the progress of its goods across international borders and deliver this tracking information to its customers. Fr8 uses it to increase transparency, building systems that use smart contracts to reduce mishaps (Stanford Online, n.d.).

Other industries, such as the energy sector, insurance, global trade, and governments, make use of the blockchain as well. IBM's Food Trust and Walmart's blockchain solution allow produce to be tracked from farm to store. The blockchain gives people a way of trading energy peer-to-peer so that they don't have to go through intermediaries like a utility company. And it can also improve the verification process for insurance claims to reduce fraud (Thompsett, 2024).

However, blockchain technology faces several pressing challenges that require attention. Scalability is one of the most significant issues. For example, today Bitcoin processes on average seven to 10 transactions per second, while Ethereum processes 15 to 30 transactions per second, both of which are far behind traditional payment systems like VISA that can do 65,000 transactions per second. This limitation makes blockchain less practical for high-demand scenarios such as global-scale payment systems or real-time financial trading. However, new cryptocurrencies such as Solana, which processes 1,000 to 3,000 transactions per second, are showing that this issue can be overcome (Chainspect, n.d.).

Another challenge is energy consumption. Blockchain networks like Bitcoin use the PoW consensus mechanism, which relies on miners solving complex mathematical problems. This process demands vast amounts of computational power and electricity, contributing to high carbon emissions. According to a study done by United Nations University from 2020-2021, the global Bitcoin mining network used about 173.42 Terawatt hours of electricity during that time period. If Bitcoin were a country, this electricity usage would rank 27th in the world, ahead of nations like Pakistan, with 230 million people (UNU, 2023).

To address these energy issues, the blockchain community has been exploring innovative solutions.

For example, sharding—a method of dividing the network into smaller, parallel processing units—and layer-two protocols, like the Lightning Network for Bitcoin, have been proposed and put into development to improve transaction speeds and capacity without compromising security. And on the energy front, many projects are transitioning to PoS, which is far less energy-intensive. Ethereum's successful switch to PoS in 2022 reduced its energy consumption by over 99 percent (Mitchelhill, 2023).

Despite these hurdles, blockchains have tremendous potential. They promise a future where trust is decentralized, transactions are secure, and access to digital resources is universal. Whether it's through applications with cryptocurrency or use in healthcare, the supply chain, or a myriad of other industries, the blockchain seems destined to stick around and change the future in many ways.

Understanding Decentralization: Promises and Challenges

Decentralization is a fundamental concept in the realm of cryptocurrency, representing a shift from traditional structures that need a central authority, such as a bank or government, to manage and validate transactions, to a more distributed network structure. This challenges the long-standing norms of centralized systems, where decisions are made by a few people who have authority. The implications extend beyond financial systems, promising a revolution in how we perceive and interact with digital and real-world environments.

In the area of finance, decentralization gives users full control over their assets. Full control is especially game-changing in regions with strict capital controls or economic instability. For instance, in a country like Venezuela, where hyperinflation has driven the value of its currency down to almost nothing, cryptocurrencies can provide an alternative that allows its citizens to access global markets and store their money somewhere more secure.

Decentralization also reduces censorship and external interference in transactions. For instance, in countries where governments restrict financial freedom, decentralized networks can enable people to send and receive funds securely and freely, ensuring financial independence.

Another major benefit is enhanced transparency and accountability. As we talked about before, blockchain transactions are recorded on a public ledger, visible to all network participants. This openness discourages corruption, fosters trust, and guarantees all participants operate with shared information.

Beyond crypto and the blockchain, decentralization fuels innovation through DAOs, dApps, and DeFi. These are all sort of similar, in that they all have decentralization at the heart of how they work, but they refer to slightly different things.

- **DAO (Decentralized Autonomous Organizations):** This refers to an organization or a group that is led by its community and members, i.e. it has no central authority. DAOs are like the decentralized equivalent of a company or a bank. Basically, it's the entity that runs something or provides some service. Uniswap is a DAO, but it's also a dApp and a DeFi service. "The DAO" is another noteworthy DAO, founded in 2016.

- **dApps (Decentralized Applications):** These are apps or software that run on the blockchain or P2P networks and are often open source, which means anyone can view the code. They can be created by DAOs, but they don't have to be. They're like the equivalent of an app that you might download on your smartphone or tablet. For instance, in the centralized world, Google is a company that creates the Google Maps app. Similarly, Uniswap is a DAO that creates the Uniswap dApp.
- **DeFi (Decentralized Finance):** This refers to financial services that are offered on the blockchain, often by DAOs through their dApps. These financial services are managed with something called smart contracts (more on that later). DeFi includes services such as trading crypto, lending crypto, borrowing crypto, earning interest, taking out a loan, and more (Akudo, 2023).

Here are some examples of DAOs, dApps, and DeFi services:

- **Crytokitties:** dApp created by a traditional company, Dapper Labs
- **Uniswap:** DAO that also creates a dApp under the same name and offers DeFi services
- **MakerDAO:** DAO that operates a DeFi service
- **OpenSea:** dApp for buying and selling NFTs, created by a traditional company of the same name
- **Friends with Benefits:** DAO that markets itself as a new kind of social network without algorithms or distractions
- **Decentraland:** DAO that operates a dApp of the same name

Decentralization in blockchain technology introduces significant challenges and risks that demand careful consideration. Governance is a primary issue because decentralized networks lack a central authority to oversee decisions or resolve disputes. This can result in stalemates or fragmentation within the crypto community. For instance, disagreements over protocol updates have led to hard forks, such as the split between Bitcoin and Bitcoin Cash, creating separate blockchains with differing visions (Reiff, 2024).

Security vulnerabilities are another major concern. Without centralized oversight, networks can become targets for coordinated attacks. One notable example is the 51 percent attack. This refers to a situation where a malicious actor might gain control of more than half of the network's computing power. This control would allow them to manipulate the blockchain, such as reversing transactions or double-spending funds, undermining trust in the system.

Additionally, the pseudonymous nature of cryptocurrencies can facilitate illegal activities, such as money laundering, ransomware attacks, and funding illicit operations. This can create regulatory challenges for governments.

Addressing these risks requires innovative approaches, such as improving governance structures, enhancing network security protocols, and developing regulatory frameworks that balance oversight with the principles of decentralization. These efforts are essential to unlocking the full potential of decentralized networks while mitigating their inherent vulnerabilities.

Key Terms Simplified: Navigating the Crypto Lexicon

DAO, DeFi, and dApps are just a few of the key terms you'll encounter as you go through learning about crypto and understanding how it all works. Here are some of the other key terms that you should know. You can also find more terms in the Glossary section at the end of this book.

- **Cryptocurrency:** This refers to any digital or virtual currencies that use cryptography for security and operate on the blockchain. Unlike the bills in your wallet, these currencies exist solely in electronic form without a physical counterpart.
- **Decentralized:** Cryptocurrencies are decentralized by nature. This means that they operate independently of a central bank, relying on nodes (computers or stakeholders) to approve transactions.
- **Digital Ledger:** Think of this like a record-keeping book for each cryptocurrency.

Transactions go on the ledger once they are approved. These transactions are grouped into blocks before they are stored on the ledger, and the size of the blocks (the number of transactions in each one) varies by the network. For instance, Bitcoin has a 1 MB block size limit, and Ethereum has a gas limit that determines the block size dynamically (Crypto 101, 2022).

- **Blockchain**: This technology is the backbone of all cryptocurrencies, but as we've seen, it can also be used in many other industries. The blockchain distributes responsibility across multiple nodes, ensuring that data remains tamper-proof and transparent. It's the method by which digital ledgers operate, and many people also use it interchangeably with the term digital ledger.
- **Mining**: In simple terms, mining is the process by which new cryptocurrency coins are created, and transactions are verified. Miners use powerful computers to solve complex mathematical puzzles, a process that validates and adds transactions to the blockchain. Successful miners earn rewards

for their efforts in the form of newly minted coins. This process both secures the network and regulates the issuance of new coins, maintaining a controlled supply. Currently, the two most popular methods of mining are Proof of Work (PoW) and Proof of Stake (PoS).

- **Wallet:** This is a digital tool that stores your public and private keys. Remember, a public key lets others send you money (akin to your address or PO Box number), whereas a private key is how you access your money (akin to the physical key for your mailbox). Unlike a real-world wallet, your cryptocurrency wallet doesn't store the currency itself but provides a way to access and manage your funds on the blockchain. Different types of wallets exist—you can classify them as either software wallets, which you download on a computer or phone, or hardware wallets, which you buy in physical form and connect to your computer in order to transact. Some examples of software wallets include Coinbase Wallet, MetaMask, Crypto.com DeFi Wallet, and Exodus. Some examples of hardware wallets include Ledger and Trezor.

- **HODL:** This is a term most often used when crypto prices are swinging wildly in the wrong direction. Crypto enthusiasts who use this term usually know that crypto will fluctuate wildly in value. Some days, Bitcoin might be up 10 percent; other days, it might be down 12 percent. HODL stands for "hold on for dear life," meaning don't sell just because the price is crashing.
- **FOMO:** This stands for "fear of missing out," and it describes the anxiety of missing potential investment gains.
- **FUD:** This stands for "fear, uncertainty, and doubt." It refers to negative information that can sway market sentiment. It might also refer to a group's collective emotions over this negative information. For instance, you might hear something about people giving in to FUD, or someone calling someone out for spreading FUD.
- **Altcoins:** These refer to any cryptocurrency that isn't Bitcoin. Ethereum is the largest altcoin by market cap, so sometimes it's excluded as well.

- **Initial Coin Offerings (ICOs):** These are methods for new projects to raise funds by selling tokens, much like how a digital crowdfunding campaign might raise money for a new product. ICOs can offer a chance for some crazy investment gains, but there are also incredible risks if you are investing in one because it means the cryptocurrency is brand new.

By familiarizing yourself with this lexicon, you'll gain the knowledge and confidence to engage in discussions, make informed decisions, and comprehend the nuanced world of cryptocurrency. This can also empower you to form connections within the crypto community and to grow your knowledge even further.

Historical Evolution: From Bitcoin's Inception to the Present

The first digital currency was called eCash. It was developed by David Chaum in 1990, but as we mentioned earlier, it didn't last. Other virtual currencies popped up between then and 2009, but it wasn't until Bitcoin was created that crypto began to really take off. Bitcoin was introduced to the world in 2008 through a whitepaper published by a person or a group named Satoshi Nakamoto. To this day, nobody knows who Satoshi Nakamoto is, and though various individuals have claimed to be him, these claims hold little merit.

Nakamoto designed Bitcoin to be a peer-to-peer electronic cash system, independent of any central authority. In his whitepaper, he provided a blueprint for a decentralized currency that could operate across borders without the constraints of traditional banking systems. This decentralized nature is a key feature of cryptocurrency today. Bitcoin's creation was both a technological innovation and a philosophical statement, challenging the conventional notions of money and financial control. On January 3, 2009, Satoshi launched the Bitcoin network, and the first block of transactions, commonly called the genesis block, was mined.

Bitcoin grew slowly at first. By the end of 2010, it was valued at just $.30 per Bitcoin. But by 2011, it began to experience more rapid growth. In June of that year, it reached an all-time high of $29.60 per Bitcoin. And then, in 2013, its value grew even more rapidly. That year it passed the $1,000 per Bitcoin mark, showing that it was more than just a gimmick.

That's when crypto hackers started to come onto the scene in a big way. In 2014, one of the biggest exchanges for buying and selling crypto, called Mt. Gox, was hacked. The hackers made away with 647,000 Bitcoins, and Mt. Gox ended up shutting down for good. Another hack occurred in 2018 when the crypto exchange Coincheck lost $530 million. Smaller hacks affected the market as well. However, what all of these hacks had in common is that they did not affect the Bitcoin network itself—they were hacks on centralized exchanges that held cryptocurrency. To date, nobody has hacked the Bitcoin network (Chaturvedi, 2025).

That's a big reason why Bitcoin has always recovered after it takes hits. As Bitcoin has grown and gained traction; additional technological advancements have followed. People have taken note of its blockchain technology, using it to improve the way digital transactions are recorded and verified across many industries. Other cryptocurrencies have followed suit, such as Litecoin, which was released in 2011 as a faster alternative to Bitcoin, and Ethereum, which came out in 2015 and revolutionized the way that cryptocurrency and the blockchain can be used. Ethereum introduced the concept of smart contracts, allowing developers to build dApps on the blockchain. The introduction of these dApps spurred widespread interest in crypto, as many new coins began to pop up in ICOs, which further diversified the market. By the end of 2017, bullish sentiment caused the market to surge, and Bitcoin led the way, reaching a high of almost $20,000 per Bitcoin (Chaturvedi, 2025). For the first time, crypto began to reach mainstream news.

Soon after, Bitcoin and other cryptocurrencies crashed due to a variety of factors. First, the surge in price was driven by an unsustainable bullish sentiment, including buy-in from many first-time crypto buyers. Second, Bitcoin was fresh off a halving from 2016, which meant that only half as much new Bitcoin was being mined and created as opposed to before the halving. And third, a large hack on the crypto exchange Coincheck in 2018 soured bullish sentiment. These factors eventually caused Bitcoin's price to come back down to as little as $3,000 per coin.

Since then, Bitcoin has experienced two more bull runs, and the market has grown with the introduction of even more new technology, dApps, and DeFi services. The year 2021 saw public sentiment shift from skepticism to cautious optimism, driven by increased awareness and understanding of the technology's potential. Crypto has received mainstream support from public figures across a variety of industries, many of which created their own NFTs when they came onto the scene in 2021. Although the regulatory landscape is murky, there are highlights as Bitcoin ETFs have been approved and companies like Coinbase have gone public and continued to thrive.

Still, one of crypto's biggest issues has been fraud and hacks. At the end of 2022, the crypto exchange FTX collapsed after it was revealed that its founder, Sam Bankman-Fried, was siphoning money from the company into an investment company called Alameda Research. This became a big problem when Alameda lost money, and it sparked the crypto exchange equivalent of a bank run. FTX went under, taking other companies in its sphere, like Blockfi, along with it. This was a huge deal in the crypto world because of how big FTX was at the time. Bankman-Fried had donated $50 million to political candidates in the 2022 elections (Schwartz, 2023), and FTX owned the naming rights to the Miami Heat's basketball arena, which was called FTX Arena from 2021-2023 (Associated Press, 2023). In early 2025, the biggest crypto hack to date occurred when $1.4 billion of Ethereum was stolen from the Bybit exchange, likely by a group of North Korean hackers (The Editors of Encyclopaedia Brittanica, 2025).

As the story of cryptocurrency continues to unfold, it's anyone's guess what the future might hold. Bitcoin and its brethren have come a long way from their humble beginnings to the diverse and vibrant ecosystem we see today. It's a testament to the power of innovation and the resilience of a community committed to a decentralized world. By understanding the historical evolution of cryptocurrency, we can gain a deeper appreciation for it and build our understanding in preparation for making informed decisions in the future.

Chapter 2
The Mechanics of Cryptocurrency

Imagine a bustling digital marketplace where transactions occur rapidly and seamlessly. This is what cryptocurrency is all about, but to get there, we need to have a method for processing transactions, and in crypto, that method is called mining.

As we discussed in Chapter 1, mining can employ either a Proof of Work (PoW) protocol or a Proof of Stake (PoS) protocol. Either way, mining involves many computers racing to solve complex cryptographic puzzles, with the winner being the one who completes the puzzles the fastest. This winner gets to add a new block to the blockchain, thereby earning a reward in the chain's native currency. For

Bitcoin, this reward is currently set at 3.125 Bitcoins per block (as of 2025).

Mining and Validation: How Transactions Get Approved

When a cryptocurrency transaction is initiated, miners receive it and pair it with other transactions, organizing them into a block. To validate the block, a miner must solve a cryptographic puzzle—a task that demands substantial computational resources. This is a crucial aspect of safeguarding the blockchain. Once a miner solves the puzzle, the solution is shared with other miners, which are commonly called nodes. When enough nodes collectively agree on the solution, called a consensus, then the block is added to the blockchain. This helps to keep the blockchain secure and reliable, as no one computer or entity can modify it without agreement from everybody.

Mining: Rewards and Incentives

Miners earn rewards in two primary forms: block rewards and transaction fees.

1. **Block Rewards:** These are newly minted cryptocurrency coins awarded to miners who successfully validate and add a new block to the blockchain. As we said earlier, Bitcoin miners currently receive 3.125 BTC per block as of 2025, but this amount is not static. Approximately every four years, Bitcoin undergoes a halving event when the block reward is reduced by half. This mechanism is designed to control inflation and ensure a finite supply, with Bitcoin's total supply capped at 21 million coins.
    - Historically, Bitcoin's halving has been a big event with the potential to start a bull run, which is a period when Bitcoin quickly increases in value. There have been four Bitcoin halving events already, with one more scheduled to happen in the future. On November 28, 2012, the block reward went from 50 BTC to 25 BTC. On July 9, 2016, it went from 25 to 12.5 BTC. On May 11, 2020, it went down to 6.25 BTC. And on April 19, 2024, it went from 6.25 to 3.125 BTC. It's currently estimated that the next and final halving will

occur in March or April of 2028, and it's likely that about 99 percent of all Bitcoin will be mined by 2032, with the last Bitcoin mining to occur sometime around the year 2140 (Swan Bitcoin, n.d.).

2. **Transaction Fees:** Miners also earn fees paid by users to process their transactions. These fees are dynamic and depend on network congestion. For instance, during periods of high activity, fees can surge as users compete to prioritize their transactions. This dual compensation model incentivizes miners while balancing network operation costs.

Environmental Challenges of Mining

The energy consumption of mining raises serious environmental concerns because much of this energy comes from non-renewable sources, contributing to carbon emissions and climate change. While the computers that are doing this work consume energy, it's ultimately the mining process that is responsible for them using all the energy, as mining is done on the computers. Critics argue that this environmental cost outweighs the benefits of mining, prompting calls for change.

Toward Sustainable Solutions

The rising energy demands and environmental costs of mining have led to explorations of alternative, more sustainable consensus mechanisms, such as PoS. Unlike PoW, which relies on miners competing to solve puzzles the fastest, PoS selects validators based on the amount of cryptocurrency they hold and are willing to "stake" as collateral. This drastically reduces energy consumption by eliminating the need for power-hungry mining equipment. As we saw earlier, Ethereum, the second-largest cryptocurrency by market capitalization, transitioned to PoS in 2022 with its "Merge" upgrade. Other cryptocurrencies like Solana have always been PoS. In Solana's case, it also uses something called Proof of History (Picardo, 2024).

Understanding Mining Pools

To mitigate some of these challenges, many miners participate in mining pools. These pools are collaborative efforts where miners combine their computational resources to increase their chances of successfully mining a block. By pooling resources, miners can achieve more consistent rewards, which are distributed based on each participant's contribution to the pool's total computational power. This also allows smaller miners to remain competitive against larger mining operations, thereby democratizing access to mining rewards and fostering a sense of community within the network.

Wallets and Security: Safeguarding Your Digital Assets

As we talked about back in Chapter 1, a cryptocurrency wallet is a digital tool designed to store your public and private keys, allowing you to send, receive, and manage your cryptocurrencies. There are several types of wallets, but in the big picture, they can all be classified as either hardware or software wallets. Hardware wallets are physical devices that store your keys offline, providing the most robust protection against online threats. Software wallets are applications installed on your computer or smartphone. They are often easier and cheaper to get started with because you don't need to purchase any new hardware. Cryptocurrency wallets can also be further categorized into hot wallets, which are connected to the Internet, and cold storage, which keeps your keys offline, away from potential cyber-attacks.

Many wallets include encryption as a key feature to protect your private keys. This is often done through something called multi-signature (multi-sig) functionality, which requires two or more private keys to approve a transaction. This reduces the risk of a single point of failure, making it harder for attackers to compromise your wallet. However, even with these protections, there are some steps you should take to make your wallet more secure.

1. **Always update your wallet software promptly** since updates often address newly discovered vulnerabilities.
2. **Enable two-factor authentication (2FA),** which adds a second verification step—such as a code sent to your phone or an authentication app—before granting wallet access.
3. **Back up your wallet data** by storing your private key or recovery phrases somewhere secure—preferably in an offline location. Many people like to write them down on a piece of paper. Just make sure that you don't

forget where you put this paper! This ensures you can restore your wallet if you lose access due to device failure or loss.

4. **Never share your recovery phrases with anyone!** If they are shared, your funds are as good as gone.
5. **Be aware that once you send crypto, the transaction is final.** Only send crypto if you're sure about the person you're sending it to. Unlike with credit or debit cards, there is no way to dispute the transaction later.

If this sounds daunting, crypto exchanges are an option that simplifies the process for some people. Unlike wallets, you don't have to worry about downloading any apps or buying any hardware. When you sign up for a crypto exchange, you're automatically agreeing to let the exchange store any crypto that you buy. This means that they're responsible for the private keys and recovery phrases, as well as keeping your money safe, similar to how a bank might keep your funds secure. The benefit is that you don't have to worry about losing your recovery phrases, forgetting your wallet information, or getting locked out. The drawback is that crypto exchanges are much more vulnerable to hacks than banks, and there are fewer protections—there is no FDIC insurance for crypto exchanges. As we've seen, that's had dire consequences for investors across many different exchanges, starting from Mt. Gox all the way to Coincheck, Bybit, and more. Similarly, there are investors who bought Bitcoin on a wallet in the early days—in some cases, it's worth millions of dollars now—and they can't get access to it because they forgot their login credentials.

Ultimately, you will need to choose the right option for you, whether that's taking a chance with a crypto exchange that you research thoroughly or picking a wallet and making a plan to keep your credentials secure. If you choose a wallet, keep in mind that hardware wallets are much more secure than software ones, and cold storage is more secure than hot storage. By understanding these intricacies, you can make much better decisions that align with what you need.

Smart Contracts: Automating Transactions in the Blockchain World

Smart contracts are a revolutionary aspect of blockchain technology that came onto the scene with the launch of Ethereum in 2015. They are self-executing programs that automate a series of actions through a set of instructions written directly into code. They operate on decentralized platforms like Ethereum, where the contract is stored on the blockchain, making it immutable and transparent. You might think of smart contracts as akin to a vending machine. When you insert money into a vending machine, it counts that money, takes your order based on which button you press, and then, if the payment is sufficient, it dispenses your chosen item. Similarly, smart contracts start with a transaction and then follow a set of pre-programmed rules according to the "contract."

Here are some use cases:

- **In real estate,** a smart contract can facilitate transactions by automatically transferring ownership of a property when payment is made.
- **In supply chain management,** smart contracts can release payments to suppliers once goods are delivered and verified.
- **For freelancers,** a smart contract can

release payment upon completion and verification of a project.

This level of automation and trust makes smart contracts a powerful tool in many industries. Once deployed on the blockchain, the smart contract becomes part of the public ledger, visible and verifiable by anyone. Execution is triggered automatically when the specified conditions are met, ensuring that all parties fulfill their obligations. This eliminates delays and any potential biases (The Investopedia Team, 2024a).

However, even though smart contracts are made from code, you don't need to know how to code to use them. If you're considering using a smart contract for your Airbnb business, for example, there are user-friendly platforms and companies that can provide services for that sort of thing. Some decentralized applications (dApps) can also offer templates for common use cases so that you can input your terms without coding. Additionally, blockchain service providers or specialized firms can help you design and deploy tailored smart contracts, ensuring they meet your business requirements without needing technical expertise.

Smart contracts offer numerous advantages over traditional agreements:

- **They reduce the need for intermediaries,** promoting efficiency and speed.
- **They reduce costs that are often present with traditional contracts** since there's less need for manual labor and administration costs.
- **Because they are stored on the blockchain,** they are much more secure than the average traditional contract. Once a smart contract is executed, it cannot be altered, providing both parties with confidence in the agreement's integrity. And the agreement is also transparent for anyone to see.

However, smart contracts are not without their challenges and limitations:

- **One significant risk is the potential for code errors and security flaws.** Since smart contracts are coded programs, any mistake in the code can lead to unintended outcomes or vulnerabilities that malicious actors could exploit. This was famously demonstrated in a 2016 hack on The DAO, where a vulnerability in a smart contract led to the theft of millions of dollars worth of Ethereum (Cryptopedia Staff, 2023). This highlights the importance of rigorous testing and auditing of smart contracts before deployment.

- **Additionally, the legal enforceability of smart contracts remains a grey area.** Traditional legal systems may struggle to interpret or enforce agreements made through code, particularly across different jurisdictions. This lack of clarity poses a challenge for widespread adoption since participants may hesitate to rely solely on code-based agreements without established legal precedents.

Despite these challenges, smart contracts hold immense potential. As blockchain technology continues to evolve, so will the capabilities and applications of smart contracts. With ongoing advancements in coding practices and regulatory frameworks, smart contracts are poised to become an integral part of the digital economy, offering a glimpse into a future where automation and decentralization redefine how we conduct business and execute agreements.

Nodes and Networks: Ensuring Decentralized Integrity

Nodes are individual computers connected to the blockchain network. Each computer maintains a copy of the entire blockchain. This is so that no single point of failure can jeopardize the network's security.

In the case of PoW systems, some nodes are operated by miners who solve complex puzzles to validate transactions and create new blocks on the blockchain. In PoS systems, validators play a similar role by staking cryptocurrency to confirm transactions. Regular users can also operate nodes to contribute to the network's decentralization and security, even if they are not actively involved in mining or validating. In this sense, all miners or validators are nodes, but not all nodes are miners or validators.

There are two types of nodes:

1. **Full Nodes:** These are the kind we've been discussing up to this point. They keep a complete, up-to-date copy of the blockchain, ensuring consistency across the network.
2. **Light Nodes:** These only store a small portion of the blockchain, which is enough to validate transactions using a simplified payment verification (SPV). Not all blockchains have light nodes. They're mostly useful for networks that operate with less storage and bandwidth. Bitcoin is one example of a network that uses light nodes (Ledger Academy, 2024).

When you operate a full node, you aren't storing multiple separate copies of the blockchain for every other user. Instead, all nodes in the network maintain their own single copy of the blockchain, and these copies are constantly synchronized with one another. For example, if the blockchain is 500 GB in size, that is the amount of space you would need as a full node—just 500 GB, not 500 GB times two or times three.

Participants within this network keep things secure by holding each other accountable. Validators in PoS systems are responsible for confirming transactions and adding them to the blockchain. Unlike PoW, which requires computational power, PoS relies on validators holding a certain amount of cryptocurrency as a stake. This stake acts as collateral, motivating validators to act honestly. If validators aren't honest, other validators will call them out, and this could potentially lead to the loss of their staked assets. Meanwhile, in PoW systems, miners who aren't honest won't get validated and, therefore, won't get any rewards or their "solved" blocks added to the blockchain.

By participating in the network, whether as a full node, light node, miner, or validator, individuals can contribute to a system that prioritizes transparency, security, and trust. In a world increasingly concerned with data privacy and security, the blockchain's decentralized architecture offers a compelling alternative to traditional centralized systems. It has systems to both safeguard digital assets and empower users with a sense of autonomy and control over their financial interactions.

Gas Fees and Transactions: The Cost of Crypto Operations

Gas fees represent the transaction costs associated with using the blockchain. Each transaction requires a certain fee, measured in units of that blockchain's cryptocurrency, which corresponds to the computational effort necessary to execute specific tasks. When you initiate a crypto transaction, you're essentially hiring the network's computational power to process and verify your request. This fee is often paid in Ethereum's native currency, ether (ETH), and is typically quoted in gwei, a subunit of ETH. Many altcoins run on the Ethereum network, so even if you're not transacting with Ethereum directly, you may end up paying gas fees in ETH. Note that if you use a crypto exchange, you likely won't see gas fees. This is because the exchange handles those fees and then passes them on to you in another form. For instance, Coinbase has its own fee structure that remains the same regardless of what cryptocurrency you're buying or selling. Binance has its own fee structure and gives users the option to pay in BNB or other currencies. Regardless, the premise is the same. Gas fees ensure that the network remains secure and efficient by discouraging frivolous or malicious activities since each action incurs a cost.

The Ethereum network operates on a fee market, where users compete to have their transactions processed quickly by offering higher fees. Miners who validate these transactions prioritize those with higher fees because the miners stand to gain more. This bidding process can cause substantial fluctuations in gas prices, especially during periods of high network activity.

The only way to manage gas costs is to be strategic about when you transact. Think about the maximum amount of gas you're willing to spend on a transaction and don't be afraid to wait if the price is too high. On the other hand, you may choose to adjust your personal limit depending on market conditions. Most exchanges will give you recommendations for how to set your gas limit to get your transaction processed. Oftentimes, you'll see a recommendation for whether you want the transaction processed fast, medium, or slow. Generally, the slow option is the cheapest, and the fast option is the most expensive. Keep in mind that any gas fee estimates you see are not final. The price may change a little bit.

Upgrades with Ethereum 2.0: A Deeper Dive

The transition to Ethereum 2.0, or Ethereum's move to the PoS consensus mechanism, was a transformative series of upgrades that enhanced scalability, security, and efficiency between 2020-2022.
Here's how:

1. **The Switch from PoW to PoS**
    - Ethereum 2.0 replaced energy-intensive PoW mining with PoS, in which validators stake cryptocurrency to validate transactions. This reduced the computational resources required, resulting in lower energy consumption and a more sustainable system.
    - Validators are now randomly selected to propose and validate blocks, significantly improving efficiency compared to PoW's competitive mining (Nambiampurath, 2024).
2. **The Introduction of Sharding**
    - Sharding divides the Ethereum blockchain into smaller segments called shards that process transactions in parallel. This drastically increases the

network's capacity by allowing multiple transactions to be handled simultaneously across different shards.
   - By spreading the workload, sharding makes the network more scalable and reduces the likelihood of congestion on any single chain.
3. **Efficiency Gains Through Reduced Latency**
   - Ethereum 2.0 has introduced a faster block confirmation process, which reduces the time it takes to finalize transactions. With increased transaction throughput, the network can handle a larger volume of activity more efficiently. Future updates aim to use something called proto-danksharding and danksharding to further increase scalability.
4. **Gas Fee Optimization**
   - With PoS and sharding in place, the network requires fewer computational resources per transaction, lowering overall gas fees for users.
   - Layer 2 solutions, such as Arbitrum and Polygon, further complement Ethereum

2.0 by reducing reliance on Layer 1 for everyday transactions, keeping costs low, and improving user experience.

As the ecosystem continues to grow and change, staying informed about gas fees and Ethereum is vital for navigating the cryptocurrency landscape effectively. Many, many applications are built on top of Ethereum today. In the next chapter, we will explore how these foundational elements integrate with broader financial systems, how you can get started with crypto, how to manage risk effectively, and how to identify scams.

Chapter 3
Investing in Cryptocurrency

Stepping into the world of cryptocurrency requires more than enthusiasm; it demands preparation and insight. As you begin, you'll need to decide whether you want to start on a cryptocurrency exchange or go straight to a wallet. Wallets are generally more secure, but they can be harder to learn to use, and if you lose your keys, you're out of luck. Exchanges serve as centralized platforms where anyone can buy, sell, and trade digital currencies. Much like banks, their role is to keep your funds safe and in your hands, so you can always go to the exchange for any issue. If you choose to go with an exchange, look for one with a solid reputation, strong security measures, and a user-friendly interface. Also, make sure to consider the exchange's fee structure, liquidity, and range of available cryptocurrencies so that you can make sure it aligns with your investment goals.

Getting Started with Crypto Investments: A Step-by-Step Guide

Cryptocurrencies are more than digital tokens; each represents a project with specific goals, technology, and real-world applications. To evaluate their potential, you must analyze several key factors thoroughly. Here's how to conduct effective research.

Evaluate the Project's Whitepaper

The whitepaper is the cornerstone of understanding a cryptocurrency project. It explains the project's vision, technology, and use cases. Pay close attention to:

- **Problem Statement:** What issue does the project aim to solve? Is the problem significant, and is the solution practical or innovative?
- **Technology:** How does the project work? Does it use blockchain uniquely or improve on existing technologies? Look for specific

technical details rather than vague promises.

- **Token Utility:** How does the cryptocurrency function within the ecosystem? Does it have clear use cases, such as governance, payments, or incentivizing behavior?
- **Revenue Model:** How does the project sustain itself? Does it outline a clear and viable financial model?

Example Resources

Websites like CoinMarketCap or CoinGecko often link to whitepapers. Alternatively, visit the project's official website directly.

Analyze the Roadmap

A project's roadmap provides insight into its short- and long-term goals. Look for:

- **Clear Milestones:** Are the timelines and deliverables realistic? For example, a project promising to revolutionize an industry within six months might be overpromising.

- **Progress:** Compare the roadmap with actual achievements. Has the team consistently delivered on past promises?
- **Development Goals:** Are upcoming updates or releases meaningful, or do they seem vague or unnecessarily delayed?

Example Resources

Projects like Ethereum provide detailed updates about upcoming developments, such as its plans around proto-danksharding and danksharding. Ethereum also has a track record of following through on its promises, such as when it released a series of upgrades to Ethereum 2.0, which lowered gas fees, transitioned the network to PoS, and increased efficiency.

Investigate the Team

You should consider the team's experience and credibility. Research:

- **Team Members:** Are they publicly known, and do they have relevant expertise in blockchain, technology, or the project's target industry? Check professional platforms like LinkedIn.

- **Past Projects:** Have they worked on successful ventures in the past, or are they associated with failures or controversies?
- **Transparency:** Is the team accessible and open about their activities? Anonymous teams may signal higher risk.

Assess Community Engagement and Partnerships

Community and partnerships can reflect a project's legitimacy and potential impact.

- **Community Activity:** Check forums, like Reddit or Quora, and news articles. Are discussions active and constructive? Are people saying good things? Watch out for overly promotional content or communities with little meaningful dialogue.
- **Partnerships:** Evaluate the project's collaborations. Partnerships with established companies, universities, or institutions often indicate credibility.
- **Developer Activity:** Review development activity on platforms like GitHub. Regular

updates and comments show an active and dedicated team.

Understand Market Data

Evaluate different sources of information that can be used to better understand a crypto's potential.

- **Market Capitalization:** A high market cap may indicate investor confidence but doesn't guarantee value. Investigate the fundamentals behind the valuation.
- **Trading Volume:** Consistent, healthy trading volumes suggest liquidity and active interest.
- **Token Distribution:** Analyze how tokens are allocated. Projects in which the majority of tokens are held by a small group (e.g., team members or private investors) could face issues of centralization or price manipulation.

Utilize Trusted Resources

When researching, make sure to take your information from reputable platforms and sources such as:

- **CoinMarketCap** and **CoinGecko**: For market data and links to official project resources
- **Messari**: For in-depth analysis and news
- **CryptoPanic**: For cryptocurrency news and updates
- **Dune Analytics**: For data visualization and metrics for blockchain projects

Beware of Scams

Look out for red flags or signs that a project might not comply with the law.

- **Red Flags**: Watch out for unrealistic promises like "guaranteed returns" or exaggerated claims without technical backing.
- **Regulatory Compliance**: Check if the project complies with regulations in your country or globally.

Conducting this level of research minimizes your chances of losing your money. The cryptocurrency market rewards informed, diligent investors who take the time to thoroughly analyze their choices.

As you venture further, adopting basic investment strategies can also help to mitigate risks and enhance your potential returns. These strategies are:

Dollar-Cost Averaging (DCA)

Dollar-cost averaging involves investing a fixed amount at regular intervals, regardless of the cryptocurrency's current price. For example, you might invest $50 weekly in Bitcoin, whether its price is rising or falling.

Why Dollar-Cost Averaging Is Effective

- **Reduces Market Volatility Impact:** Instead of risking a lump sum at a single price point, DCA spreads your investment over time, averaging out the purchase cost. This reduces the risk of buying at a market peak.
- **Eliminates Emotional Decisions:** DCA prevents emotional reactions to market swings, such as panic-selling during a dip or fear-of-missing-out (FOMO) buying during a rally.

Starting with Small Investments

Investing small amounts when you're new to cryptocurrency helps you ease into the market and learn without exposing yourself to significant financial risk.

Why Starting with Small Investments Is Effective

- **Minimizes Losses:** Cryptocurrency prices can be highly volatile, with some assets experiencing 20-30 percent price swings in a single day. On top of that, cryptocurrencies can be extremely risky—some coins will fail, and others might turn out to be "pump and dump" schemes, which we'll talk about later. Some might just not be worth as much as you think at first glance. Starting small protects you from large financial setbacks while you're still learning the ropes.
- **Promotes Learning:** With a smaller financial stake, you can focus on understanding market dynamics, such as how price movements correlate with news, market sentiment, or technological updates.
- **Builds Confidence Gradually:** Starting small lets you experiment with different platforms and strategies without feeling

overwhelmed, helping you gain the confidence to make informed decisions as you scale up.

Why These Strategies Matter

- **Discipline Over Time:** Both strategies encourage disciplined investing. DCA promotes consistency while starting small prevents impulsive, high-risk decisions.
- **Accessible to Beginners:** You don't need extensive knowledge or significant capital to implement these strategies, making them ideal entry points for new investors.
- **Long-Term Benefits:** These approaches align with the principle of gradual wealth-building. The alternative is speculative investing, when you take a big risk, especially if you don't yet have much experience in the market.

Setting clear investment goals is also important. Determine your objectives and timelines before making any investment. Are you looking for short-term gains or long-term wealth accumulation? Short-term investments might involve frequent trading and taking advantage of market fluctuations. In contrast, long-term investments focus on holding assets over extended periods, capitalizing on potential growth. Align your investment strategy with your personal financial goals. Consider factors such as your risk tolerance and financial stability. Clear goals provide direction and help you stay focused amidst the market's inherent volatility.

Investment Goals Checklist

- **Define Your Time Horizon:** Short term (a few days or a couple weeks), medium term (a few months or maybe 1-3 years at most), or long term (many years or decades)
- **Assess Risk Tolerance:** High risk, moderate risk, or low risk
- **Set Specific Targets:** How much are you willing to invest? What are your goals?
- **Monitor Progress:** Review your portfolio on a regular basis, then adjust as needed

Risk Management Strategies: Navigating Market Volatility

Cryptocurrency markets are notoriously volatile, influenced by a variety of factors that can cause rapid and unpredictable price swings. These factors can include market sentiment, often driven by current events such as new regulations, big crypto hacks, or politics, and positive developments, such as the adoption of pro-crypto policies or big investments by a major financial institution.

As of early 2025, Donald Trump's presidency has been a big cause of market fluctuations. When he was first elected in late 2024, it was seen as a positive sign for crypto by the community, as the sentiment was that he would roll back regulations. This caused the price of crypto to soar, with Bitcoin jumping to a price of over $106,000 per coin (da Silva, 2024). However, once in office, some of Trump's policies, such as his threats of tariffs on various countries, also caused downturns in the crypto market (Reuters, 2025).

Mitigating investment risk in such a volatile market requires a thoughtful approach. One key strategy is diversification, which means spreading risk across various asset classes, such as a mix of cryptocurrencies, stablecoins, and other non-crypto assets. By doing this, you can reduce the impact of a poor-performing asset on your overall portfolio.

In addition, setting stop-loss orders can be beneficial. These are automated instructions to sell an asset when it reaches a certain price, which may limit potential losses during a market downturn. For instance, in today's market in early 2025, you might set a stop-loss order for Bitcoin when it's at a price of $80,000 per coin. It has fluctuated between $85,000 and $100,000 for most of the first two months of 2025, with occasional dips, but none close to $80,000.

Managing risk will also require managing your emotions. Many people get caught up in emotional decision making, especially when prices are swinging wildly in either direction. It's easy to look at Bitcoin as it is rallying, and wish you had bought more before the rally. It's also easy to regret your buying decision when the price plummets. That's a big reason why the term HODL came about—people who use HODL are often trying to fight the temptation to make emotional decisions.

One way to fight your emotions is by setting predefined rules for buying and selling. For instance, you might agree to only buy a predefined amount every Saturday with dollar cost averaging. That way, if you get caught up in the hype surrounding a big rally on a Wednesday, you don't end up buying at the peak.

Furthermore, tools and resources for tracking and assessing risk can help you make the most out of your money. Volatility indexes can help you gauge the level of risk associated with your investments. Market analytics platforms can offer a wealth of data on price trends, trading volumes, and sentiment analysis, equipping you with the information needed to evaluate potential risks. Additionally, you can use portfolio management software to track your investments in real time and get a comprehensive view of your holdings and their performances.

Ultimately, by understanding the factors that drive volatility, diversifying your assets, and leveraging the right tools, you can approach the crypto market with confidence and clarity to make informed decisions that align with your financial objectives.

Identifying Scams: Red Flags and Safety Tips

There are many types of crypto scams, but the two most insidious ones that are commonly found in the crypto space are Ponzi schemes and fake ICOs. Both are designed to exploit the optimism and inexperience of new investors.

Ponzi Schemes

A Ponzi scheme is a fraudulent investment operation in which returns to earlier investors are paid using the funds collected from newer investors. This creates an illusion of profitability that draws in more participants who believe the scheme is legitimate.

How Ponzi Schemes Work

1. **False Promises:** Organizers often promise high, risk-free returns, sometimes claiming they are using advanced trading strategies or proprietary technologies.
2. **Early Success Stories:** Early participants are paid returns as promised and often encouraged to share their "success" to attract new investors.

3. **Collapse:** The scheme relies entirely on a steady influx of new money. Once new investments dwindle, the structure collapses, leaving later participants with significant losses.

Signs of a Ponzi Scheme

- **Unrealistic Returns:** Ponzi schemes lure in those eager for quick wealth, often with feelings of FOMO.
- **Lack of a Clear Business Model:** Ponzi schemes often lack transparency about how they will generate the promised returns. They might be vague about it or redirect your attention somewhere else, such as to the promised returns. Many Ponzi schemes will use websites that look professional, which helps redirect your attention.
- **Lack of Credible Experience:** The people running the Ponzi scheme usually don't have credible experience in the crypto or finance industries (or other industries, for that matter).

Fake Initial Coin Offerings (ICOs)

Fake ICOs are scams that fraudsters use to create fraudulent cryptocurrencies or blockchain projects to raise funds under the guise of revolutionary technology or groundbreaking ideas. Once the funds are collected, the scammers disappear, leaving investors with worthless tokens or nothing at all. Fake ICOs are often called "pump and dump." This is because those who create fake ICOs often pump up coins in value by getting people interested, and then they dump all their coins at once, selling them off at the highest price point and causing the market to crash.

How Fake ICOs Work

1. **Hype Generation:** Scammers develop flashy websites, whitepapers, and marketing campaigns to create excitement about their "innovative" project.
2. **Token Sales:** They sell tokens through pre-sales or ICOs, often accepting widely used cryptocurrencies like Bitcoin or Ethereum as payment.
3. **Exit Scam:** After collecting funds, they shut down their operations or sell all their coins, delete online presences, and vanish with investors' money.

Signs of a Fake ICO

- **Flashy Marketing with Little Substance:** Scammers often use polished websites, celebrity endorsements, or fake partnerships to appear credible. However, if you look at the underlying technology behind the coin and what it contributes to the crypto sphere, there's often not much substance.
- **Unrealistic Promises:** You might see the coin marketed as "the next Bitcoin" or offering guarantees like 10,000 percent growth.
- **Bearish Sentiment from Other Investors:** If experienced investors are wary of a new ICO, chances are you should be wary as well.

Other Scans and Threats

You should also watch out for phishing attacks and malware. These types of threats will often target you through deceptive emails, websites designed to steal sensitive information, or even texts and messages on social media apps. You should never give anyone your private keys or login credentials for a crypto wallet or exchange. Once cybercriminals obtain this kind of information, there's often little recourse for recovery. It's also a good idea to make sure that your computer and phone always have antivirus software installed. Malware can infiltrate devices through seemingly harmless downloads, so having antivirus software can be a lifeline.

Here are some examples of well-known scams that have happened in crypto since Bitcoin was first mined:

- **BitConnect (2016–2018)**: BitConnect was a Ponzi scheme that promised investors up to 40 percent monthly returns on Bitcoin. It did this by requiring that investors sell their Bitcoin for BitConnect's own proprietary coin (Garnett, 2025). Later, the company was revealed to be a Ponzi Scheme when it failed to pay out on its promises, making off with $2.4 billion in investor funds (Flipex, n.d.).
- **OneCoin (2014-2019)**: Marketed as the "Bitcoin Killer," OneCoin claimed to be a revolutionary cryptocurrency, but it had no

real-world application or underlying technology. Its creator, Ruja Ignatova, held extravagant conferences around the world to drum up interest in the coin, and once it all came crashing down, she made off with $25 billion (Somebody from Breet, n.d.). She's now on the FBI's Ten Most Wanted list (Flipex, n.d.).

- **FTX (2019-2023)**: Created by Sam Bankman-Fried, FTX was a huge crypto exchange that operated out of the Bahamas. In late 2022, it all came crashing down when another exchange's CEO, Binance's Changpeng Zhao, tweeted that he had decided to liquidate all the company's shares in FTX's token, FTT, after "recent revelations that have come to light" (Wright, 2023). This quickly caused the crypto world to investigate, revealing that Bankman-Fried was siphoning money from FTX into an investment company called Alameda Research. Bankman-Fried was eventually sentenced to 25 years in prison (Office of Public Affairs, 2024).
- **$SQUID (2021)**: This was a fake ICO with a coin inspired by the hit Netflix series *Squid*

> *Game*. Supposedly, it was going to be used in a future video game, but after collecting investors' money, the creators quickly dumped all their coins in a classic "rug pull," sending the coin to practically $0. The scammers ended up making off with $3.3 million (Somebody from Breet, n.d.).

Regulation plays a big role in mitigating scams. In many of these cases, governing bodies like the SEC or FBI have stepped up to protect investors, so this is a big reason why it's important to look for projects that comply with legal standards. Check to make sure the projects you invest in have necessary regulatory licenses and approvals, which indicate adherence to financial laws and consumer protections. Conduct background checks on project teams to verify their credentials and past achievements. This due diligence can save you a lot of money in the long run. However, in all cases, keep in mind that crypto is a risky investment, and how you choose to invest can influence the level of risk. The safest way to invest in crypto is by using a hardware wallet to purchase established coins like Bitcoin or Ethereum.

If you do fall victim to a scam, swift action is crucial. Report the incident to relevant authorities, such as the Federal Trade Commission (FTC) or the Securities and Exchange Commission (SEC), which can investigate and potentially recover funds. Engage with community support groups, who can often provide additional guidance and resources. You might be able to pursue legal recourse depending on the nature of the scam and the jurisdiction involved. While recovery is not guaranteed, these steps can increase the likelihood of restitution and help prevent future occurrences. Finally, don't be afraid to share your experience to help others avoid similar pitfalls.

Scam Prevention Checklist

- **Verify Information:** Scrutinize project details and team credentials.
- **Be Cautious with Unsolicited Offers:** Avoid clicking on unknown links or downloading suspicious files.
- **Seek Regulatory Confirmation:** Double-check that projects have appropriate licenses and approvals.

- **Report Suspicious Activity:** Contact authorities and seek community support if scammed.

Portfolio Diversification: Beyond Bitcoin to Altcoins

By spreading your investments across different assets, you can reduce risk and maximize potential returns. Bitcoin may dominate the market, but market dynamics can shift rapidly. Diversification allows you to take advantage of unique opportunities for growth, often driven by emerging technologies and innovative projects.

Many altcoins focus on solving specific problems or enhancing blockchain capabilities. For instance, Ethereum enables decentralized applications, while others like Cardano and Solana offer expanded features and efficiencies. By investing in these altcoins, you can tap into their potential and reap the rewards from any gains as they grow in popularity and use. As the crypto space evolves, these types of coins are poised to offer opportunities that Bitcoin alone cannot.

When researching altcoins for diversification, you should evaluate them carefully, using three key criteria:

1. **Market capitalization:** This figure represents how much money is invested in the altcoin worldwide. The market cap is calculated by multiplying the number of shares that exist by the value of each share. Since the value will fluctuate, the market cap can fluctuate too. If a coin's market cap is going up, that means that the coin is doing well! A higher market cap often suggests a more established project with a significant user base.
2. **Liquidity:** This ensures you can buy or sell the asset without affecting its price significantly. A coin with high liquidity is one that is being bought and sold all the time. Bitcoin has high liquidity. A coin with low liquidity is one that isn't being moved very often, which indicates that people are choosing to hold onto it for some reason.
3. **The Technology and Use Cases of the Altcoin:** You should investigate the problem that the coin aims to solve, the technology

underpinning it, and the team's capability to deliver on its promises. A strong community and active development are positive indicators. Vague details about the coin or a lack of use cases can be red flags.

Altcoins come with inherent risks. They are even more volatile than Bitcoin, which means that the gains or losses are more pronounced. Additionally, many altcoins are relatively new and lack extensive historical performance data. This absence of a track record can make it challenging to predict future movements or assess long-term viability. Market manipulation is another risk, where large holders, known as "whales," can influence prices through significant trades. Altcoins still tend to mostly follow Bitcoin's lead when it comes to daily price fluctuations. That means that on most days, altcoins are down when Bitcoin is down, and altcoins are up when Bitcoin is up.

Being aware of these risks is essential for managing your portfolio effectively. Understanding these challenges allows you to make informed decisions, minimizing potential pitfalls. By recognizing both the opportunities and risks associated with altcoins, you can navigate the crypto market with greater confidence and insight.

Analyzing Market Trends: Tools and Techniques

To understand the cryptocurrency markets, you'll need to use two main analytical approaches: fundamental and technical analysis.

Fundamental analysis involves assessing the intrinsic value of a cryptocurrency by examining the underlying factors that might influence its price. This begins with evaluating the project's whitepaper, which serves as a blueprint outlining its purpose, technology, and potential market impact. For example, projects like Polkadot and Ethereum have clearly demonstrated their value through detailed whitepapers emphasizing innovative solutions, such as cross-chain compatibility and smart contracts. Once you've assessed the whitepaper, the next step is looking at other key elements of the project, such as:

- **The Roadmap:** This includes the project's goals for the future and how it plans to accomplish those goals.

- **The Team Behind the Project:** What have they accomplished in the past?
- **How Active the Team Is:** Frequent updates and active coding efforts on platforms like GitHub are good indicators of a dedicated team working to improve the project. For instance, Cardano's consistent progress reports and peer-reviewed development approach have strengthened its position in the blockchain space.
- **Community Engagement and Partnerships:** For example, active communities on platforms like Reddit and Telegram demonstrate user interest and support, as seen with Shiba Inu. Additionally, coins like Chainlink have numerous collaborations for decentralized oracle solutions, signaling legitimacy and growth potential.
- **Market Position and Competitors:** For example, Uniswap's automated market maker model revolutionized decentralized exchanges (DEXs), distinguishing it from its peers.

Technical analysis, on the other hand, focuses on using historical price data to identify patterns and trends, helping predict future market movements. It involves several tools and techniques:

- **Chart Patterns:** These are visual formations on price charts that indicate potential market behavior.
    - **Head and Shoulders:** A pattern with three peaks, where the middle one (the head) is the highest. This is one of the most reliable signs that the market is about to turn from bullish to bearish.
    - **Triangles:** Patterns like Ascending Triangles suggest prices may break upward while Descending Triangles point to a likely downward movement (Gov, 2024).
- **Indicators:** These are calculated tools that help interpret market data.
    - **Moving Averages (MA):** These show average prices over a specific time.
    - **Relative Strength Index (RSI):** This measures whether an asset is overbought (above 70) or oversold (below 30). If Bitcoin's RSI hits 75, it may

mean a price drop is likely (Fernando, 2024b).

- **Volume Analysis:** Volume shows how much of an asset is being traded. A strong price increase with high volume suggests the movement is reliable, while low volume may signal that the price increase won't last.
- **Support and Resistance Levels:** These are price points where an asset tends to stop falling (support) or rising (resistance). For example, if Ethereum repeatedly bounces around $1,500, that level could be a strong support. When crypto prices fall past support levels, they tend to find a new support level somewhere. It's not uncommon for the old support level to then become a resistance level as crypto struggles to regain ground (Amure, 2024).

Unlike fundamental analysis, which looks at the value behind an asset, technical analysis focuses completely on price behavior and market sentiment. This means that if you want to do short-term trading, you'll probably do more technical analysis than fundamental analysis. On the other hand, if you want to do something like DCA or invest and HODL, then do more fundamental analysis, worrying less about technical analysis.

Websites like CoinMarketCap and CryptoCompare offer comprehensive data on market capitalization, trading volume, and historical performance, making them great tools for fundamental analysis. Additionally, platforms like GitHub can help you track development activity. Engaging in forums and social media channels, including Reddit and X (formerly Twitter), can provide you with insights from other investors in real-time discussions. This can be a great help with fundamental analysis, offering diverse perspectives on a project's potential.

If you are doing technical analysis, use tools such as TradingView. These tools offer a range of indicators and drawing tools to analyze price movements and patterns. You can customize your charts, apply various technical indicators to spot emerging trends and use volume analysis tools to identify trading activity that indicates whether a price move is backed by strong participation. Additionally, you can use trend lines to mark key levels of support and resistance, aiding in the prediction of future price movements.

Following industry news and expert opinions is also vital to staying informed about market developments and regulatory changes. Look for cryptocurrency newsletters run by reputable companies or join online communities that can provide regular updates and insights. Engage with communities both online and offline to share knowledge and learn from others' experiences. This collaborative approach exposes you to diverse strategies and perspectives, enhancing your ability to adapt to market shifts.

In summary, investing in crypto is a risk, but with proper preparation, you can manage that risk. This preparation involves critically assessing the intrinsic value of any coins you are going to buy, watching out for red flags that a coin or offering may be a scam, and interpreting market patterns to understand what has value and what doesn't. Whether you trade short term or long term, fundamental and technical analysis can help guide you. Remember, as you continue your exploration, diversification is the key to making the most of your money. Never invest it all in one place.

Chapter 4
Philosophical and Ethical Dimensions

Imagine a world where people are not bound by the limitations of traditional financial systems, where power is evenly distributed, and financial services are accessible to all, regardless of geography or economic status. This is the promise of decentralization—but in order to get there, we'll have to put in a lot of work. The work we'll do involves more than just developing solutions to hard problems. We also must be cognizant of how our solutions affect other people, animals, and the Earth as a whole. This is what it means to think about the ethical and moral dimensions of decentralization. We already know that decentralization shifts authority away from centralized entities, like banks and governments, to a network of peers. In doing so, it redefines how we perceive democracy, embedding it into the very fabric of our financial interactions. If we're going to implement crypto correctly, it should empower individuals by granting them control over their financial destinies. Crypto shouldn't stick people with something that limits or restricts them further.

Decentralization and Democracy: How Crypto Empowers Individuals

Decentralized systems facilitate peer-to-peer financial transactions, eliminating intermediaries that traditionally manage and oversee exchanges. This direct approach reduces costs and enhances efficiency, but more importantly, it democratizes access. In a decentralized network, decisions are made collectively, and no single entity wields overarching control. This framework is inherently democratic, allowing users to participate in decision-making processes that affect the network's future. Everyone is treated equally and without prejudice. In this way, decentralization challenges the status quo, and if we want the crypto ecosystem to remain equitable and inclusive, then we need to make sure that this vision is respected.

Similarly, cryptocurrencies can offer a gateway to financial services for millions who are unbanked, providing them with the tools to save, invest, and transact without relying on conventional banks. In developing countries where access to banking is limited or in countries experiencing severe economic hardship, cryptocurrencies have become a lifeline. For instance, many Venezuelans now use decentralized and public cryptocurrencies because their value is more secure than the bolivar (their national currency). After undergoing hyperinflation and seeing their economy collapse, Venezuelans have witnessed payment networks becoming overloaded, volatile swings in bolivar's worth—even worse than crypto swings—and difficulties with transacting in other currencies such as U.S. dollars. This means that cryptocurrencies are often the path of least resistance (Rendon, 2021). Without crypto, Venezuelans would face even more restrictions and uncertainty. This is exactly the kind of positive effect that crypto should strive to produce in the world.

Furthermore, decentralization plays a role in reducing inequality by leveling the financial playing field and providing equal access to tools previously available only to a privileged few. Think about crowdfunding platforms like Kickstarter or Indiegogo. Decentralized lending and borrowing platforms like Aave, Compound, and MakerDAO are similar. They empower individuals to lend or borrow assets without the need for a bank. That way, they can raise money for any variety of things, from startup ventures to getting a personal loan to help with rent. A borrower just needs cryptocurrency to use as collateral to secure a loan, and that loan often comes at lower interest rates compared to traditional banks. These platforms are only possible thanks to smart contracts. A lender can confidently provide funds knowing the smart contract will enforce repayment terms or liquidate collateral if conditions aren't met.

Furthermore, decentralization enables access to global liquidity pools, which means that a borrower in a developing country can secure funding from lenders across the world. This bypasses regional economic limitations and opens financial opportunities to people who might otherwise be excluded due to a lack of banking infrastructure or credit history.

These are all examples of how decentralization empowers individuals, opening up new opportunities and creating more freedom instead of restricting it. It's all about removing traditional barriers and offering more inclusive and equitable access to financial resources.

However, there are challenges. One significant concern is the concentration of wealth within the cryptocurrency ecosystem, often referred to as the dominance of "whales." As we talked about earlier, these are people who hold swaths of a coin and exert considerable influence over market prices. The whales can potentially undermine the decentralized ethos, as their decisions to buy, sell, or move their crypto from one service or provider to another can create ripple effects in the ecosystem. This also mirrors the disparities seen in traditional financial systems, which is worrying. Additionally, while tech-savvy individuals may utilize these systems with ease, those without technical expertise may find cryptocurrency too difficult to use. This can create a barrier to adoption and increased financial freedom even when people have access.

Reflection Section: Assessing Decentralization's Impact

Consider your own experiences with financial systems. Have you encountered barriers that decentralization could address? Reflect on how peer-to-peer transactions and decentralized platforms could transform your financial interactions. What challenges do you foresee, and how might you overcome those challenges to ensure widespread access and equity?

As we continue to explore the philosophical and ethical dimensions of cryptocurrency, it should be clear that decentralization is not just a technological innovation. It's a fundamental shift towards a more democratic and inclusive financial future.

Transparency in Transactions: Building Trust in a Digital Age

If the blockchain is the beating heart that keeps crypto running, then transparency is a core part of crypto's brain, dictating how it acts and communicates with the world. This communication happens transparently through something called the open ledger—in other words, a decentralized database that records every transaction in an immutable manner. If you recall, this ledger is stored independently on each computer or node, then synced on a regular basis as new blocks are added by miners or validators. The ledger is public to everyone, not just those with a node. All users and stakeholders can see transaction histories and verify the authenticity of transactions. This instills confidence in both the technology and in the entities that choose to operate within the cryptocurrency's framework, creating a more open and honest financial ecosystem.

It can also have a huge effect in reducing fraud. In traditional financial systems, the lack of transparency often allows malicious activities to go unnoticed until significant damage is done. With the public ledger, though, everyone is free to go through it. If someone is doing something shady, it's a lot harder for them to hide. Anyone in the world can see the transaction history and point it out. Moreover, smart contracts are auditable by nature. This means they can be examined by anyone, reducing the risk of manipulation or deceit. Once one person catches something wrong in a smart contract, it can quickly get reported to everyone. This not only reduces the potential for human error but also minimizes the risk of tampering or corruption, making transactions more secure and reliable.

However, while transparency is advantageous in many ways, it can also be undesirable for those who want more privacy. Blockchain transactions are pseudonymous, meaning they are not directly linked to the identities of individuals. However, if someone can link a cryptographic address to an individual, then they can track any and all money as it moves into or out of that individual's account. This can be a big issue for some people. Some cryptocurrencies, like Monero, address these privacy concerns by providing greater anonymity features, which makes it difficult to trace transactions back to their origins. Similarly, some crypto exchanges will change the address occasionally, making it harder to track transactions over the long term. These policies prioritize user confidentiality while maintaining the fundamental benefits of blockchain technology as an alternative for people who value more discretion in their financial dealings.

The blockchain can also give all of us more corporate and governmental transparency. In the corporate world, the blockchain can make the supply chain more transparent, allowing consumers to trace the journey of a product from its origin to its final destination. In the realm of governance, blockchain's transparency can revolutionize voting systems by ensuring that all votes are accurately recorded and verifiable.

As we navigate all of this, it's important to recognize the potential of transparency to reshape industries and redefine trust. Transparency is not merely a feature of blockchain; it is a transformative force that challenges traditional notions of privacy and accountability. By embracing this openness, we can build systems that are more equitable, secure, and trustworthy, paving the way for a future where trust is inherent in every transaction.

Ethical Implications: The Good, the Bad, and the Uncertain

Cryptocurrency has undeniably catalyzed innovation across various sectors. It has opened new avenues for charitable donations and created a level of transparency and efficiency unmatched by traditional methods. With cryptocurrencies, donors can track their contributions in real-time, ensuring that funds reach their intended destinations. They can also make cross-border donations more easily, bypassing the red tape that often hinders international giving. Furthermore, the rise of cryptocurrency has fueled advancements in financial technologies, pushing the boundaries of what digital finance can achieve. From the development of decentralized applications to the proliferation of smart contracts, the innovative spirit within the crypto community continues to inspire and transform industries, offering new tools and opportunities to increase opportunities and equity for the people of the future.

Despite these positive impacts, there are ethical challenges and criticisms. As we discussed earlier, one of the most pressing concerns is the environmental impact of mining operations. Cryptocurrencies like Ethereum or Solana have already addressed this by establishing or switching to PoS systems, but others like Bitcoin look unlikely to make the switch, rendering the future murky.

Another ethical challenge is the potential for financial exclusion in a space designed to promote inclusivity. While cryptocurrencies aim to democratize access to financial tools, high transaction fees often price out small-scale users, especially during network congestion. For example, Ethereum gas fees spiked in the past during peak activity, such as in 2022, when they peaked at over $400 (Young &

Baird, 2022). Needless to say, these kinds of fees make DeFi services inaccessible to many and lead to concerns that cryptocurrencies could inadvertently create a new form of inequality, benefiting those who can afford the associated costs while excluding others who cannot.

Still another ethical dilemma is that cryptocurrencies are still commonly used in illicit activities. The pseudonymous nature of digital currencies makes them attractive to criminals because people can move money without having their names tied to their public keys. This can facilitate money laundering, tax evasion, and the financing of illegal operations. While the blockchain's transparency allows for traceability, the challenge is that the decentralized and global nature of cryptocurrency networks makes it difficult for law enforcement to get much more information than that. With a bank, for instance, law enforcement can always petition it for information on an account holder. The blockchain doesn't have a central figure that can be petitioned. To combat this, many centralized exchanges are implementing stricter Know Your Customer (KYC) protocols. Governments around the world may also have a role to play in setting KYC requirements for crypto exchanges, though this will not affect wallet holders.

As we move towards the future, crypto developers and users each have ethical roles:

- **Crypto developers** have the power and responsibility to enhance security and user protection by implementing robust measures against hacking and fraud. This will probably need to include rigorous testing of platforms through both automated testing tools and bug bounty programs, such as the one used by Uniswap, which incentivizes ethical hackers with a reward of up to $2.25 million for finding and disclosing a vulnerability (Crawford, 2023). Developers must also adopt transparent coding practices by maintaining open-source repositories on platforms like GitHub. This can enable public audits and collaboration to improve system resilience. Furthermore, advanced security features, such as multi-signature wallets that require multiple approvals for transactions and hardware wallets that store private keys offline, can ensure that systems have the maximum level of security possible.

- **Users** bear significant responsibility in engaging with the crypto ecosystem ethically and securely. This means practicing proper security hygiene, such as storing private keys and recovery phrases offline, avoiding reused passwords across platforms, and enabling two-factor authentication (2FA) on all accounts. Users must also educate themselves about potential risks, including recognizing phishing attacks, fake investment opportunities, and other scams that target inexperienced participants.
- **Both developers and users** will need to advocate for more user-friendly interfaces that simplify onboarding processes. For example, wallets like MetaMask and platforms like Coinbase have worked to streamline the user experience and reduce barriers for newcomers. This is especially important when users aren't tech-savvy. Additionally, supporting education initiatives like Binance Academy or CoinGecko Learn can help demystify

complex cryptocurrency concepts, which opens crypto up to a wider audience.

When it comes to ethical concerns, regulatory frameworks play a big role in addressing the concerns in a lasting way. Regulators will need to balance innovation with consumer protection and craft policies that foster growth while safeguarding users from potential pitfalls and scams. A big part of this will be developing ethical guidelines for ICOs, so that these fundraising mechanisms are conducted transparently and fairly, protecting investors from fake coins or pump-and-dump schemes. Furthermore, regulators must consider the broader implications of cryptocurrency on economic systems and devise strategies that don't have a negative effect on everyday people's finances or livelihoods. This will probably involve ongoing dialogue between governments, industry stakeholders, and the public.

Real-World Blockchain Applications: Beyond Currency

Beyond cryptocurrency, the blockchain has many different applications. In this section, we'll look at those applications in depth:

- **Healthcare:** The blockchain is revolutionizing how patient data is managed. Medric:M, a transparent peer-to-peer ledger, is a decentralized record management system that allows providers to track files and information and uses smart contracts for automated forms. It also allows patients to easily control who has access to their health information, ensuring compliance with HIPAA laws. Similarly, IBM and Walmart have developed blockchain technologies for pharmaceutical providers. Their solutions allow pharmacy products to be tracked end-to-end, reducing counterfeit medications and improving processes during recalls or quality issues (Reiff, 2025).
- **Intellectual Property Rights:** Artists, musicians, and creators often struggle to secure their intellectual property in a digital world where copying and piracy are rampant. The blockchain offers a transparent and immutable record of ownership for creators to establish and prove their rights unequivocally. For example, platforms like Rarible, OpenSea,

and Foundation enable artists to tokenize their work as NFTs that prove authenticity and ownership. These tokens are recorded on the blockchain, ensuring that the original creator is always recognized even if the work changes hands. At present, the U.S. Patent and Trademark Office (USPTO) receives hundreds of thousands of new trademark applications every year (Rossow, 2018). By adapting Intellectual Property (IP) law to work with the blockchain rather than ignore it, we can make the process of trademarking, copyrighting, and patenting more meaningful and efficient.

- **Licensing and Royalty Distribution:** Musicians can use platforms like Royal or Audius to tokenize their music, granting fans the ability to own a share of their songs while ensuring royalties are automatically distributed through smart contracts. Similarly, platforms like Sound.xyz offer blockchain-based solutions for managing music licensing, ensuring fair compensation for creators every time their work is used, along with options for buying or selling the songs through NFTs.

- **Supply Chain Management:** The blockchain increases transparency, allowing stakeholders to monitor the movement of goods from production to delivery. Businesses can verify the authenticity of products and ensure that they meet quality and ethical standards. This helps combat counterfeit goods and strengthens consumer trust. For instance, the German startup Tracifier provides supply chain services that integrate the blockchain into their processes. Tracifier is built on top of the Oracle Blockchain, which is used to authenticate the validity of transactions, automate smart contracts, and give customers greater transparency. This ultimately reduced food processing costs for Tracifier's customers by 40 percent (Chen, 2024b).
- **Real Estate:** The blockchain is streamlining property transactions by digitizing records and enabling smart contracts. These automated contracts reduce the need for intermediaries, such as lawyers and brokers, thus lowering costs and expediting the process. Buyers and sellers can complete

transactions more efficiently, with greater certainty about the accuracy of property records (Liebkind, 2020).

- **Finance:** DeFi platforms, which run on the blockchain, are disrupting traditional finance models. They're doing this by reducing the time and resources required to execute contracts, minimizing the potential for disputes and errors. Beyond these decentralized solutions, many traditional companies are integrating the blockchain into their processes. VISA, for instance, launched VISA B2B Connect in 2017, which uses the blockchain for international business-to-business payments. Meanwhile, Chase Bank uses a system called Kineys Digital Payments, which is built on top of blockchain infrastructure (Daly, 2025).

However, the path to widespread blockchain adoption is not without challenges. Scalability remains a significant hurdle since current blockchain networks often struggle to handle a high volume of transactions at a speed comparable to traditional systems. This issue can limit their applicability in large-scale operations. Integration with existing systems also poses difficulties, requiring businesses to adapt their infrastructure and processes to accommodate the blockchain's idiosyncrasies. To overcome these challenges, we'll need community engagement and user adoption. Successful projects often invest in educating stakeholders about the benefits of blockchain, encouraging a sense of ownership and commitment to the technology's success. And in addition, ethical issues like crypto's environmental impact, the risk of excluding certain groups because of high network fees, and the dangers of the blockchain being used for illicit activities will present difficulties.

While the blockchain offers unparalleled transparency and security, its success depends on addressing technical, ethical, and social challenges. The journey towards full integration will require collaboration between innovators, regulators, and users. As we move forward, we'll use what we have learned to look at the role of cryptocurrency in modern finance, examining how it can become a seamless part of our everyday transactions.

Chapter 5
Cryptocurrency in Modern Finance

Cryptocurrencies operate on decentralized networks, which fundamentally contrasts with the centralized control of traditional fiat currencies issued by governments and managed by banks. Decentralization removes intermediaries, allowing for peer-to-peer transactions that are faster and often less expensive than conventional methods. However, did you know that decentralized technologies can work hand-in-hand with traditional, centralized services? It doesn't have to be a competition.

In previous chapters, we looked at ways that centralized corporations can use blockchain technologies. The use cases for cryptocurrency and decentralized services extend beyond the blockchain. In traditional finance, central authorities govern the flow of money, adjusting policies like interest rates and money supply to maintain economic stability. However, cryptocurrencies manage these kinds of issues on their own. That can be extremely powerful.

Cryptocurrency vs. Traditional Finance: A Comparative Study

Two of the most significant advantages of cryptocurrencies over traditional financial systems are the speed and cost of transactions. Digital currencies built on top of the blockchain operate around the clock, unhindered by the limitations of banking hours or geographic boundaries. This constant availability results in near-instantaneous settlement times, a stark contrast to the multi-day processing typical in traditional banking. Santander Bank, which has already implemented blockchain solutions in its money transfer processes, is a great example of how this can change banking. In 2018, it launched Santander One Pay FX, which makes it possible for customers in many countries to transfer money internationally and have it received on the same day (Santander, 2018).

Additionally, the transaction fees associated with cryptocurrencies are generally lower because they bypass the need for intermediaries like banks or payment processors. Citibank, for instance, generally charges $35 if you're sending a wire transfer and $15 if you're receiving one. On top of that, there are sometimes fees from intermediary banks that you're required to pay. By contrast, crypto transactions are generally way cheaper. Online exchanges usually charge between 0.4 percent and 1 percent for crypto transactions, or if you trade through a DeFi service with your wallet, then you just pay the gas fee. We discussed gas fees previously, but did you know that they vary wildly depending on what cryptocurrency you're trading in? For Bitcoin, the gas fee is often just a few dollars (OneSafe Content Team, 2024). For Litecoin, it's even cheaper—it usually just costs a few cents.

This reduction in costs benefits both individuals and businesses, particularly those engaged in international trade, where exchange rates and transfer fees can significantly impact profitability. For central banks, the use of blockchain technology for international transfers has the potential to bring down costs and speed up processes for their customers as well.

Despite these benefits, cryptocurrencies face limitations that hinder their ability to fully replace traditional finance. Volatility remains a prominent issue; prices are subject to rapid fluctuations that can thereby inflate costs. This unpredictability poses significant risks for both investors and everyday users. Furthermore, governments are still grappling with how to regulate crypto, which means there isn't an easy solution to keep users' funds safe from market crashes or fraud. Many blockchain networks, if not all, struggle with the issue of scalability. As we saw in the previous chapter, existing payment systems are much faster than blockchain networks when it comes to how many transactions they can do per second. VISA, for instance, is capable of up to 65,000 tps (transactions per second). Bitcoin averages 7-10 tps and Ethereum 10-15 tps. At present, a cryptocurrency called Internet Computer is the fastest crypto network. It has been recorded on Chainspect doing up to 25,000 tps. Solana is also frequently talked about for its high transaction speed. It has been recorded doing up to 2,900 tps.

Despite these challenges, the potential for synergy between cryptocurrencies and traditional finance is immense. Hybrid financial products that combine the strengths of both fiat and digital currencies are gaining traction. Stablecoins like USD Coin (USDC) by Circle and Tether (USDT) are pegged to traditional assets like the U.S. dollar, offering users the price stability of fiat currencies while benefiting from blockchain's speed and cost-efficiency. These stablecoins can be used for seamless cross-border payments, remittances, and DeFi activities without the volatility typically associated with cryptocurrencies.

On top of that, major institutions like JPMorgan Chase have started creating their own centralized versions of cryptocurrencies. JPMorgan Chase created JPM Coin to make transactions available 24/7 (Ledger Insights, 2024). Similarly, Santander uses blockchain technology for international transfers, reducing processing times from days to mere hours. These advancements demonstrate how blockchain's secure and transparent ledger can revolutionize transaction processing by eliminating intermediaries and reducing costs.

Additionally, tokenized assets, which represent ownership of real-world assets like stocks, bonds, or real estate on the blockchain, are creating new investment opportunities. Platforms like Tokeny and tZERO allow for fractional ownership, providing users with greater access to traditionally illiquid assets.

These are just some of the ways that traditional and digital finance can be combined to create a more efficient, complementary ecosystem. Traditional finance brings the stability, trust, and regulatory frameworks that cryptocurrencies lack, while blockchain-based solutions enhance speed, transparency, and accessibility. Together, they offer users a broader range of choices, bridging the gap between two financial worlds.

Reflection Section: Evaluating Financial Ecosystems

Consider how cryptocurrencies could fit into your financial life. How might you leverage the benefits of both traditional and digital financial systems to change the ways you send money, receive money, borrow, invest, or save? What challenges or opportunities do you foresee in integrating these systems? By contemplating these questions, you can better understand the evolving landscape of finance and identify where cryptocurrencies might play a role in your future.

The Role of Central Banks: Bridging Old and New Systems

Central Bank Digital Currencies (CBDCs) represent a transformative step in the evolution of the financial system. They combine the stability of state-backed currencies with the efficiencies of digital innovation. CBDCs are designed to function as a digital equivalent of cash, offering real-time transactions without the need for intermediaries. This significantly reduces transaction costs and delays, particularly in cross-border payments. Some examples include the Bahamas, which created the Sand Dollar, and China, which created the Digital Yuan.

Beyond efficiency, CBDCs hold the potential to revolutionize monetary policy implementation. By leveraging programmability, central banks can design digital currencies to directly influence money supply and demand. This capability offers more precise tools to manage liquidity, control interest rates, and implement targeted economic policies, such as directing stimulus payments toward specific sectors. For instance, programmability could ensure that government aid is spent on essential goods rather than saved, amplifying its intended economic impact. However, the adoption of CBDCs also presents challenges. Central banks must navigate complex regulatory laws to seamlessly integrate CBDCs with existing financial systems while maintaining stability. Balancing innovations with robust privacy protections and ensuring compatibility with traditional banking systems will be critical to fostering trust and achieving long-term success.

Some of the challenges that central banks will likely face include:

- **Balancing Innovation with Financial Stability:** The rapid adoption of digital currencies could disrupt established financial institutions and markets. Central banks must ensure that the introduction of digital currencies does not compromise the stability of the financial system, which requires careful planning and regulation.
- **Addressing Privacy and Security Concerns:** While digital currencies offer

transparency, they also pose risks related to data privacy and cybersecurity. Central banks must implement robust measures to protect against unauthorized access and maintain users' privacy. This involves developing secure infrastructure and establishing clear guidelines on data usage and protection.

Looking to the future, central banks must adapt to coexist with cryptocurrencies. Collaborations with fintech companies present opportunities for innovation and growth in this area. By partnering with technology firms, central banks can leverage cutting-edge solutions to offer better digital products. These collaborations can facilitate the development of innovative financial products that combine the stability of traditional currencies with the flexibility of digital assets. Additionally, the adoption of blockchain technologies for central banking functions could revolutionize how central banks operate. Blockchain's transparency and security can enhance central banks' ability to monitor and manage financial transactions, providing greater oversight and reducing the risk of fraud.

DeFi: Revolutionizing Financial Services without Banks

Decentralized finance (DeFi) represents a groundbreaking shift in how financial services can be delivered to people. Unlike traditional finance, which relies on centralized institutions like banks and brokers, DeFi operates on blockchain networks, offering services such as lending, borrowing, and trading without intermediaries. DeFi is all about offering these services to people who don't have access under the current system. At its heart is the concept of peer-to-peer lending and borrowing. This means users can lend their digital assets to borrowers and earn interest, while borrowers can access loans swiftly without the extensive paperwork or credit checks typically required by banks. This peer-to-peer model democratizes access to financial services, enabling anyone with an internet connection to participate in global finance free from geographic or bureaucratic constraints.

Decentralized exchanges (DEXs) form another cornerstone of DeFi. Remember when we talked about the differences between DAOs, dApps, and DeFi? Well, DEXs are another part of the decentralized ecosystem that encompasses all these things. DEXs are akin to dApps that provide banking features. Think about Paypal, Venmo, Cashapp, or even Apple Pay or Google Pay. These are the centralized equivalents of DEXs, but DEXs offer many more features beyond the ability to send or receive money. By using smart contracts, DEXs provide a secure and transparent environment for trading digital assets. This eliminates the need for trust in a central entity, and instead, you're putting your faith in the reliability and integrity of the smart contract's code and the blockchain.

DeFi platforms do not require extensive documentation or proof of identity, making them excellent options for the unbanked and underbanked populations. In most cases, the only requirement is that if you want to borrow money, you must put up crypto as collateral. This means that many more people will end up qualifying for DeFi services than qualify for traditional banking services. This inclusivity extends to small businesses and entrepreneurs who can leverage DeFi to raise capital, manage assets, and conduct transactions efficiently. By removing the gatekeepers of finance, DeFi has the potential to spur economic growth and innovation on a global scale.

Despite these advantages, it's not without risks and challenges. One of the primary concerns is the vulnerability of smart contracts to exploits. While smart contracts are designed to execute automatically when certain conditions are met, flaws in the code can be exploited by malicious actors, leading to significant financial losses. One prime example is the attack on The DAO that we discussed earlier. This underscores the importance of rigorous testing and auditing of smart contracts before deployment. Similarly, regulatory uncertainty also poses a significant challenge. While well-written smart contracts have clearly enforceable rules, it's less clear how well those rules could hold up in a court of law.

Looking ahead, DeFi holds immense potential to reshape the financial world. Integration with traditional financial institutions could bridge the gap between centralized and decentralized systems, creating a hybrid model that leverages the strengths of both. As DeFi matures, it could expand into new markets and services, offering innovative solutions for asset management, insurance, and more. The continued evolution of DeFi will depend on the development of robust regulatory frameworks and the resolution of technical challenges. Only time will tell whether DeFi becomes a central pillar of the global financial system or whether it continues to occupy the niche it currently occupies.

Crypto's Impact on Global Economies: Opportunities and Threats

Like many new technologies, cryptocurrencies bring a wealth of opportunities that can reshape the job market. In the blockchain and crypto sectors, job creation is on the rise. Many companies worldwide are adopting blockchain technology, and they need professionals skilled in development, security, and analytics. These new roles are set to bolster economies and provide workers with well-paid, high-tech jobs that can lead to increased financial security and innovation. Additionally, cryptocurrencies are set to enhance financial inclusion, offering access to capital for those who traditional banks often overlook. This has the potential to allow more individuals and small businesses to secure funding and participate in the global economy as entrepreneurs. In turn, this increase in entrepreneurs can stimulate economic growth, adding yet more jobs and reducing inequality.

In fact, we're already seeing the rise of a whole new job sector thanks to crypto. Websites like cryptojobs.com, web3.career, and cryptojobslist.com have a plethora of jobs in the sector, ranging from engineering to marketing, customer service, design, and even legal jobs. Some employers pay their employees in crypto, making cross-border paychecks much easier. Web3.career gives job seekers the option to sort by jobs that pay in crypto, with companies like Tether, P2P.org, and Seedify listed.

However, the widespread adoption of cryptocurrencies also poses significant threats to global economies, especially if crypto continues to grow unchecked. This would create an environment ripe for speculation and volatility, leading to asset bubbles and subsequent market crashes, similar to how the stock market crashed after the dot-com bubble burst.

Additionally, on a geopolitical level, cryptocurrencies can influence global power dynamics by impacting national monetary policies and potentially enabling sanctions evasion. Because digital currencies operate independently of central banks and pseudonymously, they can undermine a government's ability to control its money supply and implement monetary policy effectively. This can pose a threat to national sovereignty, as traditional tools for managing economic stability become less effective.

Finally, as with many new technologies, crypto will likely do away with as many jobs as it creates. As the blockchain grows in use across new brands and industries, banks and other financial service providers will find themselves without a need for many of the intermediaries they had before. It will be up to these people to reskill or upskill in a new area, and it will be up to all of us, collectively, to help them as they do that.

Insurance and Cryptocurrency: Protecting Your Investments

As the cryptocurrency ecosystem expands, insurance can play a big role in increasing investor confidence. Insurance of crypto assets can protect against losses from theft, hacking, and smart contract failures, similar to a safety net for investors who have to deal with these threats. As we've seen, attacks on crypto providers aren't going away. From the attack on Mt. Gox back in 2014 to the person who took advantage of an error in The Dao's smart contract to enrich himself to the hack on Coincheck and the recent incident with Bybit, it seems like nothing will stop people from looking for a way to take advantage of the system. Companies like Evertas offer specialized insurance products designed to address these unique risks, from digital asset theft to technological errors in platform operations. In fact, Evertas specializes in crypto insurance, which means it pays attention to the evolving nature of crypto assets.

The challenge of insuring crypto, however, is that it is inherently volatile. Unlike traditional assets with value that can be appraised based on historical data and market trends, cryptocurrencies often lack a consistent historical framework for risk assessment. This makes it difficult for insurers to accurately price policies and evaluate potential liabilities. The value of insured assets can change dramatically within short periods. For instance, one day, an insurer might quote $20 a month to insure your Bitcoin. If Bitcoin doubles in value, that $20 suddenly might not cover it anymore. Insurers will need to address these challenges by developing innovative risk assessment models that account for volatility, ensuring that coverage remains relevant and effective.

Ultimately, as digital assets become more mainstream, insurance seems destined to play some kind of role. It's a huge safety net that enhances investor confidence and encourages broader participation in the crypto economy. By protecting against unforeseen events, insurance can help stabilize the market and contribute to its long-term sustainability. For investors, having insurance coverage means peace of mind and knowledge that their assets are safeguarded against potential threats. This assurance is vital in building trust within the crypto ecosystem, fostering an environment where innovation and growth can thrive.

As we move on to the next chapter, we'll take what we learned about crypto and modern finance and how they can work together and add to that information with new skills to conduct technical analysis more effectively.

Chapter 6
Advanced Investment Insights

In crypto, technical analysis is the study of graphs, charts, and patterns to make predictions about how prices might change in the future. It's mostly used when making short-term trades, so not everyone will need to know it. If you're the kind of person who likes to buy and HODL, then you're not going to be using technical analysis. If you have a packed schedule taking care of your kids, putting in 40-plus hours a week at your day job, and keeping up with your household responsibilities, then you may not have time to engage in technical analysis. However, if you dream about trading crypto to support yourself, then this stuff is for you. Technical analysis isn't 100 percent certain. In the world of crypto, anything can happen. But for investors who want to think crypto day in and day out, it's an art that is crucial for making informed decisions in a volatile market.

Technical Analysis for Crypto: Reading the Charts

At its core, technical analysis involves studying historical price data to predict future market behavior. By examining chart patterns and indicators, you're aiming to identify trends and potential reversal points. This approach rests on the belief that historical price movements tend to repeat themselves, as influenced by market psychology. In this section, we'll talk about crypto market indicators, including signs such as the Head and Shoulders, Double Tops, Bollinger Bands, and Ascending/Descending Triangles. TradingView, Binance, and Coinbase Pro are all great websites to use when conducting technical analysis. As we go through these patterns and strategies, feel free to follow along by examining the chart of your favorite cryptocurrency.

Moving Averages

Moving averages are one of the most commonly used tools in technical analysis. They help traders see the bigger picture by smoothing out daily price fluctuations and showing the overall direction of an asset's price over time.

There are two types of moving averages:

1. **Simple Moving Average (SMA):** The SMA is calculated by adding up the prices of an asset over a specific number of days (e.g., 10, 50, or 200) and dividing by that number.
   - **Example:** If the prices over the past 5 days are $10, $12, $14, $16, and $18, the five-day SMA is ($10 + $12 + $14 + $16 + $18) ÷ 5 = $14.
   - **Why It's Useful:** This is useful because it gives you an average price over a period, making it easier to see whether the price is trending up, down, or sideways.
2. **Exponential Moving Average (EMA):** The EMA is like the SMA, but it gives more importance to recent prices, making it react faster to price changes.
   - **Example:** If the price suddenly spikes, the EMA will adjust more quickly than the SMA to reflect the change.

- ◦ **Why It's Useful:** Since the EMA is designed to draw attention to the most recent changes in an asset's price, it's a great tool for spotting short-term trends.

Moving averages aren't just used in crypto. They can also be used when trading stocks, looking at real estate prices, or evaluating the values of just about any asset that fluctuates in value. Moving averages are useful for spotting trends in the prices of these assets. If the price stays above the moving average, it's a sign of an uptrend (prices are generally rising). If the price stays below the moving average, it's a sign of a downtrend (prices are generally falling) (Fernando, 2024a).

During an uptrend, prices often "bounce" off a moving average line. This line is commonly called the support level. This is because it helps to keep the asset's price up. When the price gets close to the support level, it often triggers many buyers to purchase the asset, causing it to go up in price again. In a downtrend, a similar thing happens in the other direction. The moving average line is called a resistance level, and when the price gets close to the resistance level, it causes sellers to shed the asset, driving prices lower.

The golden cross and the death cross are two patterns that technical analysts commonly use when assessing the moving average. A golden cross happens when a short-term moving average (like a 50-day SMA) crosses above a long-term moving average (like a 200-day SMA). This signals a possible price increase and a bull market. Meanwhile, a death cross happens when a short-term moving average crosses below a long-term moving average. This signals a possible price drop and the start of a bear market (The Investopedia Team, 2024b).

By using some of these indicators, including SMA for a broader view and EMA for quick updates on short-term changes, you can make more confident decisions, even if you're new to trading.

Relative Strength Index (RSI)

We already talked about RSI in Chapter 3, but here we'll discuss it in more detail. Remember, the RSI is a tool that helps traders figure out if an asset, like a cryptocurrency or stock, might be overvalued or undervalued based on recent price changes. It gives a score between 0 and 100:

- **Overbought (Above 70):** If the RSI goes above 70, it means the asset has been bought a lot recently, and its price might be too high. This could lead to a drop in price soon.
    - **Example:** If Bitcoin's RSI hits 75 after a big price jump, it might mean the price is due for a correction or pullback.
- **Oversold (Below 30):** If the RSI falls below 30, it means the asset has been sold a lot, and its price might be too low. This could lead to a price rebound.
    - **Example:** If Ethereum's RSI drops to 25 after a sharp decline, traders might see it as a chance to buy before the price recovers.

The RSI can be used alongside many different indicators to make predictions about the market. Here are some examples:

- **The RSI is going down, and the price is going up.** This is called a bearish divergence, and it could mean the price is about to drop.

- **Example:** A stock's price keeps hitting new highs, but the RSI starts to drop, signaling that the upward momentum is weakening.
- **The RSI is going up, but the price is going down.** This could mean that the price will soon rise because more people are starting to buy the asset.
- **Example:** Ethereum's price drops lower, but the RSI starts rising, signaling a possible recovery.
- **The RSI stays high (above 70) for a while without reversing.** This could signal a strong uptrend because it indicates powerful buying momentum.
- **The RSI stays low (below 30) for a long time.** This could indicate continued selling pressure because there are not a lot of people buying the asset.

By looking at RSI values and combining them with other indicators like moving averages, you can get a better idea of whether to buy or sell, making RSI a great analysis starting point (Fernando, 2024b).

Bollinger Bands

Bollinger Bands are a tool for understanding how volatile the market is and identifying possible buying or selling opportunities. They consist of three lines drawn on a price chart: a middle band and two outer bands.

1. **Middle Band (SMA):** This is a 20-day simple moving average (SMA). It acts as a base for the other two bands.
2. **Upper Band:** This is calculated by adding two standard deviations to the middle band, representing the higher price range.
3. **Lower Band:** This is calculated by subtracting two standard deviations from the middle band, showing the lower price range.

The outer bands move closer together (contract) when the market is calm and farther apart (expand) when the market is volatile. They are mostly used as a secondary indicator to confirm the results from other analysis methods, such as the MA or RSI. Here are some examples of how to use Bollinger Bands:

- **Overbought Signals (Upper Band):** If the price touches or moves above the upper band, it may mean the asset is overbought, and the price could soon drop.

  - **Example:** If Bitcoin's price touches the upper band after a steady rise, it could signal that the price is too high and might pull back.
- **Oversold Signals (Lower Band):** If the price touches or moves below the lower band, it might mean the asset is oversold, and the price could rise.
  - **Example:** If Ethereum's price hits the lower band after falling for several days, it could signal that it's undervalued and might bounce back.
- **Breakouts:** When the price moves outside the upper or lower band, it shows that the market is making a strong move. However, this doesn't tell you the direction of the next trend, so it's important to look at other signals.
  - **Example:** If Solana's price closes above the upper band with high trading volume, it could signal the start of a new uptrend.
- **Reversals:** If the price touches one band but doesn't break through, then moves back toward the middle band, it could mean the trend is reversing.

    - **Example:** If Dogecoin touches the upper band but fails to go higher and then starts moving down toward the middle band, it could be a sign the uptrend is weakening.
- **Bollinger Band Squeeze:** When the bands come close together (a squeeze), it shows the market is very quiet and not much is happening. This usually means a big price move is coming soon.
    - **Example:** If Ripple's (XRP) bands tighten and the price suddenly breaks above the upper band, it could signal the start of a strong upward trend.

In Simple Terms

- When the price is at the **upper band**, it might be too high (overbought).
- When the price is at the **lower band**, it might be too low (oversold).
- When the bands get very **close together**, something big might happen soon.

Bollinger Bands are a great way for beginners to visualize market activity and make better decisions about when to buy or sell (Thompson, 2024).

Head and Shoulders Pattern

As we talked about in Chapter 3, the Head and Shoulders pattern is a reliable reversal formation. This means that when you see it, it signals a shift from bullish (uptrend) to bearish (downtrend) sentiment or vice versa. The pattern has three parts to it:

1. **The Head:** The highest peak in the middle.
2. **The Shoulders:** Two smaller peaks on either side of the head.
3. **The Neckline:** A line drawn across the base of the peaks, acting as a key support or resistance level.

In an inverse Head and Shoulders pattern, the peaks will instead be dips. For instance, you might see a coin's price dip by five percent, recover, dip by 10 percent, recover again, and then dip another five percent before recovering one final time and then breaking through the resistance level (Gov, 2024).

Double Tops and Bottoms

These are patterns that are usually seen over a longer period of time, but visually, they are similar to the Head and Shoulders. The difference is that Double Tops don't have a middle peak. They just have two peaks (or dips) that are roughly the same height. In many cases, the second peak will be slightly below the first as buyer sentiment wanes and resistance hits the market.

1. **Double Top:** Formed when the price hits a high (resistance level) twice but fails to break through, suggesting the uptrend is weakening, and a downtrend may follow.
    - **Example:** If Bitcoin's price hits $30,000 twice but then drops below the neckline, it may indicate a bearish reversal.
2. **Double Bottom:** Opposite to a Double Top, this pattern occurs when the price hits a low (support level) twice and then rises, suggesting a bullish reversal (Chen, 2024a).

Ascending and Descending Triangles

Triangles are continuation patterns, which means that they serve as indicators that the market will resume its current trend after a brief consolidation. There are two types of triangles:

1. **Ascending Triangle:** Formed when the price fluctuates between rising support levels but fails to break through a resistance level. This is a strong indicator that the price will soon break out in a big way.
   - **Example:** If Ethereum's price forms higher lows at $1,500, $1,520, and $1,540 while resistance holds at $1,600, a breakout above $1,600 may indicate further price increases.
2. **Descending Triangle:** The opposite, when lower highs form against a consistent support level, often leading to a downward breakout.
   - **Example:** If Bitcoin's price makes lower highs at $89,600, $89,000, and $88,000 while support holds at $85,000, a break below $85,000 could signal a further decline (Gov, 2024).

Why Chart Patterns Matter

By identifying these patterns, you can anticipate potential market movements, making the most of your short-term trades. However, be careful. Just because you know the patterns doesn't mean that you will always spot them correctly. For instance, it's common for a Double Top to look like an Ascending Triangle before it fully forms. If you don't identify this correctly, you might invest, thinking the price is about to break out before it goes in the opposite direction! It takes time and experience to become good at spotting the patterns.

Also, be aware that technical analysis has its limitations and risks. One big challenge is the possibility of market manipulation and false signals. In crypto, large investors known as "whales" can make huge trades that create misleading patterns, which form as a result of the whale's crypto movement and not the market's trading. Relying too much on technical indicators without looking at real-world factors, like news or economic changes, can lead to wrong predictions. These events can affect prices in ways that technical analysis alone can't predict.

To handle these challenges, combine technical analysis with a basic understanding of the market and current events. It's also important to know that understanding cryptocurrency investment takes time. With its ups and downs, the market can be unpredictable, and learning often comes with both gains and losses. That's why it's a good idea to start small. Making smaller investments gives you the chance to learn and improve your skills without risking too much, which will help you feel more confident as your knowledge grows.

Interactive Element: Chart Pattern Recognition Exercise

To strengthen your skills in interpreting technical indicators, try the following exercise:

1. Review historical price charts and identify at least three of the patterns discussed: Head and Shoulders, Double Tops, and Ascending Triangles.
2. On a piece of paper, write down when these patterns occurred, which cryptocurrency they occurred in, the conditions under which they emerged, and the subsequent price movements. Look at real-world events that were happening at the time.
3. Write down something you learned about how these insights could inform your trading strategy.

By mastering technical analysis and integrating it with broader market insights, you position yourself to make smarter, more precise, and more confident decisions in crypto trading. As you refine your skills, remember that the key to successful trading lies in adaptability, continuous learning, and a balanced approach that considers both technical and fundamental factors.

Understanding Market Sentiment: Bullish vs. Bearish Trends

Market sentiment reflects the collective mood of investors and traders towards a particular asset or the market as a whole. It can be categorized into two main trends: bullish and bearish. A bullish sentiment indicates optimism, with investors expecting prices to rise. In contrast, a bearish sentiment suggests pessimism, where the expectation is for prices to fall. These sentiments directly impact supply and demand in the cryptocurrency market, thereby influencing prices.

You can effectively gauge market sentiment by using several different techniques and tools. One widely used method is the Crypto Fear and Greed Index, which quantifies market emotions on a scale from 0 to 100. Low scores indicate extreme fear, while high scores suggest extreme greed. The index analyzes various metrics, including volatility, market momentum, and social media sentiment, to provide a snapshot of prevailing market attitudes. You can access it on many different websites, especially those that are geared towards crypto price tracking. CNN has a great tracking tool for the index that also reveals historical values, including one week, one month, and one year ago. Data from the index can be combined with technical analysis strategies to better identify market tops and bottoms, triangles, Head and Shoulders patterns, and other crypto price movements.

Additionally, analyzing social media posts is a great way to gauge the public's sentiment in real time. If people on platforms like X (formerly Twitter) and Reddit are spreading FUD, it can indicate bearish activity. Conversely, if people are getting excited about something in the crypto world, it can indicate the start of a bullish trend. However, if you track social media activity, be sure to filter out noise and focus on meaningful discourse. If something is getting attention in a very niche group, such as a forum devoted to a small cryptocurrency like Monero, it may not have much of an effect on the wider market.

Another potentially effective strategy is contrarian trading. This involves going against prevailing sentiment. The logic is that markets often overreact to extreme emotions like fear or greed, creating opportunities for traders to profit from corrections. For instance, when the market exhibits extreme greed—indicated by tools like the Crypto Fear and Greed Index or widespread FOMO—prices can become overvalued. Contrarian traders may anticipate a downturn and sell or short the asset, expecting a price correction as market enthusiasm cools. Conversely, during periods of extreme fear, when prices drop sharply due to panic selling, contrarian traders might see an opportunity to buy undervalued assets, expecting a rebound when sentiment stabilizes (Chen, 2022).

To be successful with contrarian trading, you'll have to gain experience in analyzing the market, and you'll need to be precise about executing your trades. You'll also need to have a will of steel when it comes to tuning out all the emotions from crypto's wild price swings. This requires patience, discipline, and a strong understanding of sentiment dynamics, but it can be highly rewarding when executed effectively.

At the end of the day, sentiment analysis has its limitations. Relying solely on it can lead to pitfalls since it may not always accurately predict market movements. It works best when combined with other tools and strategies, such as technical and fundamental analysis. By integrating these approaches, you can become more confident and knowledgeable about dealing with the complexities of the cryptocurrency market, enabling you to make the right trade more often.

ICOs and Token Sales: Opportunities and Risks

ICOs are how new cryptocurrencies and the technologies behind them raise money. Unlike traditional stock or ETF Initial Public Offerings (IPOs), ICOs offer tokens, which can serve various purposes depending on their type. These tokens are typically classified into two main categories: utility tokens and security tokens.

Utility Tokens

Utility tokens provide access to a product, service, or ecosystem within a specific project. They are not designed as investments but rather as functional tools. For example:

- **Basic Attention Token (BAT):** This is a utility token that is designed to reward users of the Brave browser and content creators. Users earn tokens by viewing ads, which can then be donated to content creators that the user likes.
- **Filecoin (FIL):** Holders of FIL can use it to pay for decentralized storage services on the Filecoin network.

At present, utility tokens are often unregulated and are not considered financial securities, but they must still comply with relevant laws to avoid being misclassified (Coinbase, n.d.-b).

Security Tokens

Security tokens, on the other hand, represent an investment in a project or company. These are very similar to traditional securities like stocks or bonds. Holders may receive benefits such as dividends, profit sharing, or voting rights. Because they function like investments, security tokens are subject to stricter regulations, such as securities laws enforced by authorities like the SEC (Coinbase, n.d.-b).

For investors, participating in an ICO can mean getting in on the ground floor of a promising new technology or platform. This can lead to huge returns on your investment—for instance, Polkadot experienced huge growth after its ICO. It originally offered coins at a price of $0.29 each. By 2020, the price was up more than $4 a coin. Additionally, ICOs are an avenue to support innovative projects that transform industries. By investing in these ventures, you play a role in their development, potentially shaping the future.

However, there are risks. Depending on where ICOs are established and where you live, they might fall under securities regulations, requiring them to comply with strict legal standards and making investing more complex. Furthermore, ICOs can lead to the loss of your investment just as easily as they can lead to gains. As we talked about earlier, there are lots of fake ICOs out there that are just aimed at getting your money. These frauds and scams dilute the market and can be hard to spot. On top of that, legitimate ICOs are difficult for the average investor to study. A lot of knowledge about crypto is required to determine which coins actually have sticking power and which might fail to achieve mass adoption.

To tackle these complexities, approach each opportunity with a critical and methodical analysis. Use the tools and strategies we discussed in Chapter 3 to make well thought out decisions. Examine the project from multiple angles and take your time. Start small and diversify.

Additionally, assess the tokenomics of the project, including:

- **Token Utility:** How will the token be used within the ecosystem? Does it have a real purpose, such as powering transactions, enabling governance, or accessing services?
- **Supply Distribution:** How are the tokens allocated? If a high percentage is reserved for founders or private investors, that could lead to centralization or price manipulation.
- **Hard Cap and Fund Allocation:** How much does the ICO aim to raise, and how will funds be allocated (e.g., development, marketing, or legal compliance)? Overly ambitious funding goals or unclear allocation plans could signal poor planning.

By applying rigorous evaluation criteria and maintaining a healthy skepticism, you can approach the ICO landscape in a smarter way and identify projects that offer both innovation and potential returns while mitigating risk.

Leveraging DeFi: Yield Farming and Staking Explained

In the world of DeFi, yield farming and staking are two popular ways to earn passive income. These strategies allow you to make money from your digital assets without actively trading. Here's how they work:

1. **Yield Farming (aka Liquidity Mining):** You can do this using a DeFi platform, such as Uniswap or PancakeSwap. First, you'll need to deposit your cryptocurrency into a liquidity pool on your chosen platform. These pools ensure there's enough cryptocurrency available for traders to swap between assets. In return for providing liquidity, the platform will give you rewards, such as additional tokens (e.g., UNI or CAKE) or a share of the transaction fees

paid by traders. While this offers the potential for high returns, it comes with big risks. If the value of your deposited tokens decreases, you can lose a huge portion of your investment—called impermanent loss. Since yield farming often requires you to lock up your crypto for a certain amount of time, you may not have the opportunity to sell. In addition, bugs in a smart contract's code or issues within the liquidity pool that you're a part of can cause even more severe losses.

2. **Staking:** This involves locking up your cryptocurrency on a blockchain that uses a PoS system, such as Ethereum 2.0 or Solana (SOL). By staking, you help validate transactions and secure the blockchain network, earning rewards in the form of more cryptocurrency. Staking typically offers a more stable and predictable income compared to yield farming, as it is less affected by market volatility. Platforms like Coinbase, Binance, or blockchain wallets like Phantom Wallet allow you to stake your assets with ease. However, staking often comes with lock-up periods, during which

> you cannot withdraw your funds, and in some cases, there may be minimum staking requirements. For example, staking Ethereum independently on Ethereum 2.0 requires 32 ETH, though exchanges like Coinbase or Binance allow smaller amounts by packaging multiple users' ETH together to meet the minimum requirements.

In the past, some exchanges offered other methods for earning interest on crypto. For instance, Blockfi, Celsius, and Voyager are three exchanges that at one time offered investors the opportunity to join interest programs. These programs promised a regular return in the form of interest on any crypto that an investor held in their account. Companies generated this interest through a variety of methods; however, the strategies they used ultimately exposed them to significant risks. When crypto neared the bottom of its bear market in the middle of 2022, Celsius and Voyager went under. Later, when FTX was revealed to be fraudulent, Blockfi followed suit.

Investors ultimately lost money because they had to wait for their funds to be repaid in bankruptcy. Even in cases like Blockfi, which repaid 100 percent of funds to most investors, it was repaid based on the crypto's price at market bottom. That means that if someone held 1 BTC when Blockfi went under in November of 2022, they might have only ended up with 0.3 BTC afterward, as Bitcoin more than tripled in price from 2022 to 2024. The collapse of these companies was a stark reminder of the danger of holding crypto in a centralized exchange. Many people within the community responded with the catchphrase, "Not your keys, not your wallet," reminding the world that the power of crypto comes from its decentralized nature.

To navigate challenges like these, employ strategic approaches to yield farming and staking. Diversification is a key principle—don't keep all of your crypto on one platform or in one protocol. By diversifying, you mitigate the risk of a single point of failure and can capitalize on varying returns offered by different projects. Furthermore, regularly monitoring performance and adjusting allocations are equally crucial. Keep track of market conditions, reward rates, and the overall health of the protocols involved, then use that data to make quick decisions. Monitor social media, relevant news articles, and online forums to make sure that you get the news as quickly as possible. For instance, crypto investors who were aware of news as Blockfi crashed may have been able to move their funds from an interest account to a wallet account to lessen any losses.

As you explore the intricacies of yield farming and staking, view them as part of a broader strategy within your cryptocurrency portfolio. These DeFi practices not only offer avenues for passive income but also support the underlying infrastructure of the crypto ecosystem. By understanding their mechanics and associated risks, you can engage with these strategies more effectively, aligning them with your investment goals and risk tolerance. As DeFi continues to evolve, staying informed and adaptable will be key to leveraging these opportunities and succeeding in the world of decentralized finance.

Chapter 7
Addressing Skepticism and Building Trust

Have you ever heard someone say that Bitcoin has no value? When people first started hearing about it, many of them doubted that it would ever amount to much. Back in 2017, when it surged to almost $20,000 per coin, there were still doubters. Even now, many view it as a speculative bubble waiting to burst. Warren Buffett, for instance, has previously said things like, "I can say with almost certainty that [cryptocurrencies] will come to a bad ending." and that crypto is "probably rat poison squared" (Mohamed, 2022).

These kinds of comments represent the other side of crypto hype. When so many people are saying different things, it can be hard to know who to believe. Critics might say things like cryptocurrencies lack inherent value, that without physical backing, they're mere illusions, or that they don't produce anything. However, this misses the point. Like fiat money, cryptocurrencies derive value from the belief and trust of their users. Their value is not intrinsic but is supported by scarcity and utility within technological ecosystems.

In this chapter, we'll look at some of these skeptical narratives and myths. Keep in mind that many of the well-known products and technologies we use today started from a place of skepticism and distrust. In 1902, an article in the *New York Times* called the automobile impractical. When dialogue was first introduced in films, many doubted that audiences would like it (Edwards, 2015). In the 1980s and 1990s, there were people who doubted the internet would last. Robert Metcalfe, the inventor of Ethernet, said it would "go spectacularly supernova and in 1996 catastrophically collapse." Astronomer Clifford Stoll said, "No online database will replace your daily newspaper" (Russell, 2013). Nowadays, these statements have proven false, illustrating the fact that we never really know what the future holds.

Debunking Myths: Separating Hype from Reality

One common misconception in the world of cryptocurrency is that it's a path to getting rich quickly. Enthusiasts often point to stories of early investors or people who took big risks that panned out as examples. For instance, back in 2021, amid a bull run, there was a story about a Dogecoin investor who became a millionaire by investing his life savings (Browne, 2021). Other stories share how people have bought houses or funded vacations with crypto earnings. While it's true that some have profited, these narratives overlook the volatility and risks inherent in the market. Historical price trends reveal significant fluctuations, with periods of rapid gains followed by steep declines. A study from the Bank of International Settlements in 2022 showed that the vast majority, from 73 percent to 81 percent of new crypto investors, lose money on their initial investment (Barr, 2022). We just don't hear about those losses in most cases because they aren't big news. That's why it's important to proceed with caution. Invest slowly, learn, and don't expect overnight success. It's all about understanding market dynamics and investment strategies.

Critical thinking is also important when navigating cryptocurrency information. You must approach this space with a discerning mindset. Evaluate sources for credibility and cross-reference information with multiple outlets. Not all sources are reliable. Distinguish between credible ones and people who are just speculating or spreading sensational ideas. By doing this, you can form a well-rounded understanding of cryptocurrency's role in modern finance, free from the distortions of myth and hype.

Reflective Exercise: Evaluating Cryptocurrency Information

Use the following exercise to practice evaluating cryptocurrency news.

1. **Identify a Recent Cryptocurrency News Story:** Choose a news article or post related to cryptocurrency.
2. **Evaluate the Source:** Determine the credibility of the source. Is it a reputable publication or an unverified social media account?
3. **Cross-Reference Information:** Compare the story with at least two other sources. Do

they corroborate the facts, or are there discrepancies?

4. **Analyze the Tone:** Consider whether the tone is objective or sensational. Is there an agenda driving the narrative?
5. **Reflect on Your Findings:** Write a brief summary of your analysis and how it shaped your understanding.

Balancing Perspectives: Revolution or Speculative Bubble?

As we talked about at the beginning of the chapter, many people view cryptocurrency as a bubble that could pop at any moment. Is there any truth to this? Only time will tell, but crypto is already revolutionizing the world in a variety of ways:

- **Increased Financial Inclusivity:** Digital currencies are providing banking access to the unbanked, allowing people in regions with limited financial infrastructure to participate in the global economy. Additionally, they're challenging traditional banking systems by bypassing intermediaries, reducing transaction costs, and offering faster cross-border payments.

- **Major Investors:** Nations like El Salvador have embraced Bitcoin as a legal tender, showcasing a bold step towards integrating digital currencies into daily life. Major corporations, including Tesla and MicroStrategy, have also invested heavily in Bitcoin, signaling institutional confidence.
- **Blockchain Utility:** As we've talked about, companies across a wide swath of industries, from healthcare to e-commerce to real estate, are incorporating the blockchain into their processes to make things more efficient and reliable.

On the flip side, there are reasons to believe a bubble might exist. Many people make historical comparisons to the dot-com bubble, which eventually wiped out a lot of money from the market, though much of the technology remained. The crypto market's notorious volatility and susceptibility to price manipulation also add fuel to these concerns. It's easy to be concerned about a cryptocurrency's long-term viability when all of them fluctuate in price so drastically, moving as much as

15 percent in either direction in a day. And then there's the scalability problem that we talked about earlier. That's a huge issue.

As you navigate this debate, you'll need to form your own opinion. Consider your individual risk tolerance because investing in cryptocurrencies requires a stomach for volatility and uncertainty. Align your decisions with personal financial goals and values. Are you seeking long-term growth, or are you drawn to the thrill of short-term gains? Your answers to questions like these should guide your approach.

Media Narratives: How News Shapes Public Perception

Another big driver of skepticism, distrust, sensationalism, and hype is the media. Many websites and advertisements use clickbait that's crafted to capture attention, regardless of whether the content is balanced or factual. Articles may focus on dramatic fluctuations in Bitcoin prices, presenting them as either catastrophic losses or unprecedented gains, without providing the context necessary to understand these movements. News might also focus on what is happening when an event occurs, such as a new regulation or a big company making a notable investment, without focusing on the why. This approach can skew public perception, instilling unrealistic fear or optimism. Prominent media outlets have the power to amplify these narratives, impacting market sentiment on a large scale.

For example, when Tesla announced it was purchasing several Bitcoins and adding them to its portfolio of assets, as well as its decision to allow customers to purchase cars in Bitcoin, it drove prices up. When the SEC approved Bitcoin ETFs for the first time, it had a similar effect, inspiring headlines describing it as a "watershed moment" or a "boon for the crypto industry." (Yaffe-Bellany, 2024). Conversely, negative media coverage has induced panic. As we've seen, stories highlighting big crypto hacks or fraud in the industry (in the case of FTX) have led the market to experience downturns. Such narratives can cause investors to react emotionally rather than rationally, leading to market volatility. FTX's crash, while it affected many in the community, had no effect on Bitcoin's underlying technology or the reliability of Ethereum's smart contracts. Still, it sent prices plummeting.

As you assess the information out there, you'll need to have a critical eye so you can examine and extract the "why" out of news articles that you read. Cross-referencing news with official announcements can also help verify the accuracy of the information and the influence of current events. Official statements from regulatory bodies are generally the most reliable, followed by communications from companies. Also, consider whether the story is driven by an agenda, such as promoting a particular investment or viewpoint. In some cases, articles may leave something unsaid that would completely change the nature of the news. Once you pay attention to these things, you can make more informed decisions that lead you to make better trades and invest in more worthwhile cryptocurrencies.

The Future of Regulation: What to Expect

As cryptocurrency continues to integrate into mainstream finance, it's inevitable that it will become more regulated. Currently, the regulatory environment is a patchwork of policies that significantly differ across jurisdictions. In the United States, the SEC and the Commodity Futures Trading Commission (CFTC) play pivotal roles in overseeing digital assets, each focusing on aspects like securities and commodities, respectively. Notably, the administration of President Donald Trump (in his second term) is reducing regulatory burdens on cryptocurrency companies and boosting digital asset adoption through looser regulations than when former President Joe Biden was in office.

Meanwhile, the European Union is advancing Markets in Crypto-Assets Regulation (MiCA), a comprehensive framework aimed at harmonizing regulations across member nations. It allows providers of digital wallets and other crypto services to market and sell their products in the EU, provided they register with national authorities and meet certain minimum guarantees to safeguard investors. Parts of MiCA went into effect in 2023, with the rest of it rolling out at the end of 2024. As of early 2025, it is fully applicable in all member states (Nevil, 2024).

In Asia, countries have embraced a patchwork of different regulations, depending on the country. Japan, for instance, is one of the most crypto-friendly countries. The Financial Services Agency (FSA) views it as a type of money and legal property. There aren't any restrictions on owning or investing in crypto. Contrast that with countries like China, which has banned cryptocurrency mining. Meanwhile, Thailand and Singapore have some regulations but are friendly towards crypto. Dubai in the UAE is working on becoming a global hub for the crypto technology. The UAE set up a whole regulatory body, Dubai's Virtual Assets Regulatory Authority (VARA), which acts as a watchdog for the city, supporting policies that the country enacts like Know-Your-Customer (KYC) procedures and Anti-Money Laundering (AML) strategies (Kaur, 2023).

Looking forward, the regulatory landscape is poised for significant evolution. Comprehensive frameworks should provide clearer guidelines that balance innovation with the need for oversight. These frameworks will need to emphasize consumer protection. The rise of CBDCs is also influencing regulatory strategies as governments seek to integrate digital finance within existing monetary systems. The key will be establishing a regulatory architecture that supports the burgeoning crypto economy while mitigating risks associated with fraud and instability.

Trust and Legitimacy: Building Confidence in Crypto

Transparency is a cornerstone in blockchain operations. As we've seen, the blockchain needs to be open and immutable—that way, all transactions are recorded and verifiable by anyone. This transparency reduces the possibility of manipulation and fraud, providing a solid foundation for trust. Furthermore, technological advancements have the potential to bolster trust through enhanced security. Hardware wallets and multi-signature transactions make digital assets and exchanges safer, securing the community against cyber threats. These are examples of advancements that play a vital role in building trust; however, there is still a way to go.

As we talked about at the start of this chapter, there is still a lot of FUD about whether crypto has a future as a currency or even an asset. In addition, the lack of regulation often makes the crypto community look a bit like the wild west of finance. One initiative that can help with all the fear and uncertainty is the adoption of best practices and standards. Collaboration with regulatory bodies to expand regulations across the world and streamline policies can help people to feel more secure in their investments and to trust the blockchain more.

In particular, the industry will need to address the recurring, high-profile cases of exchanges being hacked and fraudulent projects disappearing with investor funds. These are incidents that need to be minimized, and need to have a plan in place for when they happen. In addressing these unethical incidents, the perceived lack of accountability and governance within the crypto space poses a significant hurdle. Unlike traditional financial systems, which have established oversight mechanisms, cryptocurrencies often operate in decentralized environments with limited intervention. This can lead to a lack of recourse for investors in cases of fraud or misconduct. The same decentralized nature that many benefit from also shows its downside in these situations, suddenly looking like a double-edged sword.

To get through this, we'll need to come together and advocate for ethical practices, regulation, and transparency that will take the industry to the next level. By championing such values, we can contribute to a culture of trust and integrity within the community.

Ultimately, transparency, security, and collaboration are the elements that will underpin success as we proceed toward a new future with cryptocurrency at the helm. While challenges will always remain, the progress being made already is encouraging. We can get there! In the next chapter, we'll explore how these elements integrate into the broader financial ecosystem by examining the transformative potential of cryptocurrencies and blockchain technology to reshape the future of finance.

Chapter 8
Real-World Cases and Applications

Have you ever heard the term "digital gold?"

If you have, you've probably heard it uttered in the same sentence as Bitcoin. And there's a good reason why. Bitcoin has emerged as a formidable store of value, much like gold. They both share a scarcity that underpins their value—gold through its physical rarity and Bitcoin through its capped supply of 21 million coins. Bitcoin's rollout in 2009 marked a radical shift from the tangible to the intangible. It didn't start out as something that aimed to be like gold, but that's what it has become. While its history is considerably shorter, its potential as a hedge against inflation is becoming increasingly recognized, with its price reaching unprecedented heights as investors seek to own a part of the first technology built on the blockchain.

Bitcoin as Digital Gold

Major corporations and financial institutions are beginning to acknowledge Bitcoin's potential as a reserve asset. Asset management firms and the approval of Bitcoin ETFs have opened the doors for more traditional investors to enter the cryptocurrency space. These developments not only validate Bitcoin's status but also reflect a shift in how financial entities perceive digital currencies. By integrating Bitcoin into their portfolios, these institutions are doing what people in the past used to do with gold. They're collecting it as a hedge against future financial uncertainties and embracing the value it adds to their business.

Central banks, once skeptical, are now grappling with the implications of Bitcoin's popularity as well. Its rise has prompted many, such as Blackrock, to make investments in the space. Even President Trump has spoken about the possibility of buying Bitcoin as a reserve asset (Macheel, 2025). This illustrates a significant shift in monetary strategy. Physical gold was once used to back the U.S. dollar. In the future, a U.S. Bitcoin reserve could support the economy in a similar way, lending strength to the dollar or any CBDCs that are developed.

However, despite its promise, there are some obstacles to Bitcoin becoming an asset similar to gold. Its price volatility can deter risk-averse investors, as dramatic fluctuations challenge its role as a stable store of value. Additionally, environmental concerns related to Bitcoin mining have sparked debates about sustainability. The energy-intensive process of mining Bitcoin, driven by the PoW consensus mechanism, may lead to problems related to its carbon footprint. Even though it is similar to gold, crypto still has a very short history. It's been around for less than 20 years—gold has been around for millennia.

Reflection Section: Bitcoin vs. Gold

Consider the parallels and differences between Bitcoin and gold. Reflect on how each asset has been perceived historically and in the present day. What do these perceptions tell us about their roles in the future of finance? As you ponder these questions, think about your own views on Bitcoin's potential as digital gold. How does its digital nature shape your perception of its value compared to traditional assets like gold?

Ethereum and Smart Contracts: A New Era of Innovation

Ethereum's smart contracts have a diverse range of real-world applications. Here are some examples of how these smart contracts are being used now and will be used in the future:

- **Bee Token:** This is a dApp that is addressing the issue of property rentals with a decentralized solution akin to Airbnb. With Bee Token, users can rent a room or a bed and pay in crypto, dodging the fees that centralized services like Airbnb are forced to charge (Schiller, 2018).
- **Smart Contracts in Insurance:** In the insurance industry, smart contracts have the potential to streamline claims processing by verifying policy terms and triggering payouts automatically when conditions, such as verified damages, are met. This reduces administrative overhead, minimizes disputes, and speeds up the settlement

process for policyholders. Smart contracts could eventually be used in everything from health insurance to property insurance (Rapal, 2024).

- **Voting Systems**: As the blockchain is transparent and immutable, smart contracts eventually could be used to secure voting systems. They would make excellent, natural solutions to mitigate fraud and create a more trustworthy electoral process.
- **The Gaming Industry**: Smart contracts could be used to enable the creation of unique digital assets as NFTs, allowing players to own, trade, or sell in-game items with guaranteed authenticity. They could also make it easier for users and creators to track rights, as well as owners or creators to collect royalties (Sharma, 2024).

Ethereum is not resting on its laurels. The platform is undergoing significant changes to enhance its capabilities and address existing limitations. Ethereum 2.0 has already rolled out. More changes are coming, with the introduction of danksharding and improvements to the scalability of the network. These advancements are expected to make

Ethereum more robust and accessible, paving the way for broader adoption and innovation.

There are also some additional obstacles. Because smart contracts are immutable once deployed, any errors in the code can lead to costly exploits, as demonstrated by high-profile incidents like the DAO hack, where a flaw in the code was exploited to siphon approximately $60 million worth of Ethereum from the decentralized organization. To overcome this obstacle, the industry will need to take a look at more robust coding practices and more rigorous audits in the development of smart contracts. Developers must test and audit smart contracts to ensure their security and reliability before they are put to use.

Along with this, the legal recognition and enforceability of smart contracts remain areas of concern. Traditional legal systems are still adapting to the concept of code-based agreements, which can create uncertainty for parties relying on smart contracts for critical transactions. This lack of legal clarity poses challenges for broader adoption because users may hesitate to engage with smart contracts without established legal precedents.

As Ethereum evolves and addresses its challenges, it stands poised to further disrupt traditional systems, offering a glimpse into a future where transactions are not just digital but inherently smarter and more secure.

Crypto in E-commerce: Transforming Online Transactions

In e-commerce, cryptocurrencies can offer us multiple benefits that traditional payment methods struggle to match. This includes advantages such as:

- **Reduced Transaction Fees:** Digital currencies often bypass the high costs associated with credit card processing and banking fees. This cost efficiency is particularly appealing to online retailers seeking to maximize profits, especially in competitive markets.
- **Faster Settlements:** Traditional banking systems can take days to clear transactions, whereas cryptocurrency payments settle within minutes, improving cash flow for businesses and providing instant gratification for consumers.

- **Global Accessibility:** By transcending borders and eliminating the complexities of currency conversion, digital currencies enable seamless cross-border transactions. This opens doors for businesses to tap into international markets and attract more tech-savvy customers who prefer digital payments.

Several e-commerce platforms are already embracing cryptocurrencies, setting the stage for broader adoption. Major players like Overstock and Newegg have integrated Bitcoin and other digital currencies as payment options, signaling a shift in how online retailers approach transactions. Expedia also accepts Bitcoin as payment for travel bookings, and Microsoft allows consumers to buy their digital products with Bitcoin as well. These are just the tip of the iceberg (Pacheco, 2024).

Understanding consumer behavior and attitudes towards crypto is important for businesses aiming to capitalize on the crypto trend. In the future, businesses will need to be more cognizant about how their customers want to pay and use that information to adapt and grow. As awareness and familiarity with cryptocurrencies increase, so too will the likelihood of their integration into mainstream shopping habits, driven by consumer demand for innovative and flexible payment options.

The future of these technologies in e-commerce holds immense potential. As more businesses recognize the advantages of digital currencies, the development of crypto-friendly payment gateways is likely to accelerate. These gateways can streamline the process of accepting and processing cryptocurrency payments, which makes it easier for retailers to integrate digital currencies into their existing systems.

Additionally, stablecoins could play a pivotal role in minimizing volatility for transactions. By pegging their value to fiat currencies, stablecoins offer the stability that traditional cryptocurrencies lack—a reliable medium of exchange for both consumers and merchants. This stability is essential for building trust and encouraging widespread adoption. As the e-commerce landscape continues to change and grow, it wouldn't be surprising to see stablecoins emerge as a promising way to conduct online transactions, offering a glimpse into a future where digital currencies are as ubiquitous as credit cards and PayPal.

NFTs: Value and Opportunities Beyond Art

NFTs experienced huge growth during the 2020-2021 crypto bull run. Unlike cryptocurrencies such as Bitcoin or Ethereum, which are interchangeable and identical to one another, NFTs represent unique digital assets. Each NFT has its own distinct value, much like a rare painting or a limited-edition collectible. They utilize blockchain technology to provide a verifiable record of ownership and provenance, ensuring that each asset is one-of-a-kind. This characteristic has propelled NFTs into the spotlight, capturing the imagination of artists, collectors, and investors alike.

While NFTs initially gained fame in the art world, their potential extends far beyond that. In the real estate sector, for example, NFTs can tokenize property deeds, simplifying transactions and ownership transfers. In the realm of intellectual property rights, NFTs offer a secure and transparent way to prove ownership and monetize creative works. In gaming, NFTs have transformed how players interact with virtual items. Players can buy, sell, and trade in-game assets, creating a vibrant marketplace that extends beyond the confines of individual games. Even identity verification can be improved with NFTs, which offer a decentralized way to manage your personal data and credentials.

Recently, the fashion industry has been exploring how to use NFTs to bridge physical and digital experiences. For instance, Alice Delahunt, former chief digital officer of Ralph Lauren and founder of the fashion startup Syky, released an NFT drop in 2023 that combined access to both digital and physical events, as well as other perks (McDowell & Schulz, 2023). Along similar lines, the tourism sector is adopting NFTs to enhance visitor engagement. Jeju Island in South Korea plans to launch an NFT-powered visitor card aimed at attracting young tourists, which demonstrates how NFTs can be utilized to offer unique and interactive travel experiences (Kumar, 2025).

These examples illustrate the expanding applications of NFTs across various industries, showcasing their versatility in creating innovative solutions beyond the art world. However, despite all the opportunities, the NFT market also faces some big challenges.

One of the main issues is how quickly prices can change. Like cryptocurrencies, NFT prices can be volatile, swinging from one level to another in the blink of an eye. This can be risky for creators, who might not earn as much as they expect, and for buyers, who might lose money if the value of their NFTs drops suddenly.

Another challenge is determining copyright and ownership. Sometimes, people take digital art they don't own and turn it into NFTs without permission. This can cause confusion about who really owns the rights to the art or the NFT. Also, because digital art can be easily copied, it's not always clear what makes an NFT special or original.

These challenges underscore the need for robust legal frameworks and technological solutions, such as blockchain-based copyright registries and advanced content verification systems, to protect creators, ensure fair compensation, and maintain trust in the NFT ecosystem.

Looking ahead, the future of NFTs is filled with intriguing possibilities. Integrations with virtual and augmented reality platforms are one possibility. They could provide immersive experiences where users can see and interact with NFTs in new ways. Cross-chain NFT marketplaces are also a strong possibility. They would allow for the seamless transfer of NFTs across different blockchain networks. These advancements could increase liquidity and accessibility, making NFTs more user-friendly and appealing.

Chapter 9
Future Trends and Innovations

Imagine a world where artificial intelligence (AI) and blockchain technology merge. With its ability to process vast amounts of data and learn from patterns, AI could complement the blockchain's immutability and transparency. Or how about a world where using the blockchain is much less energy intensive? In the future, more networks could use solutions like PoS to drive down energy costs and create a greener earth. Have you heard of the metaverse? Imagine that we've integrated it into our daily lives. Your ownership of real-world assets is reflected in the metaverse. It's a place that you can go to interact with your community, exchange ideas and build new growth. These are the kinds of frontiers that cryptocurrency is moving towards right now. In this chapter, we'll look at how these kinds of future technologies can revolutionize industries, make operations more efficient, and pave the way for a more connected world.

Emerging Technologies: AI and Blockchain Synergies

In the future, AI marketplaces could provide a space where algorithms and data sets are freely exchanged without the need for intermediaries. These marketplaces would enable developers and businesses to access AI resources, fostering innovation and collaboration. They'd also serve to decentralize access to AI, enabling anyone, especially smaller players, to compete in the space. For instance, imagine a data scientist in one part of the world seamlessly purchasing a developer's algorithms or code and using the blockchain's transparent, secure environment to create a new, groundbreaking product or service. This is the kind of thing that an AI marketplace integrated with the blockchain would be able to achieve. It would encourage diverse perspectives and ideas to drive the next wave of technological advancement.

AI-driven automation could also improve efficiency and accuracy in smart contracts. With AI, future smart contracts could autonomously audit themselves, identifying discrepancies or potential failures before they occur. Remember when we talked about the dangers of bugs or errors in smart contract code? With AI, we could reduce or even eliminate these errors, removing much of the need for manual oversight. Consider a decentralized insurance contract that can automatically assess claims based on predefined conditions and historical data. AI-powered analytics within the contract could evaluate the legitimacy and risk associated with each claim, streamlining processes and reducing fraud. This seamless integration of AI into blockchain operations would ultimately increase trust and reliability, which are both key components for widespread adoption.

Furthermore, AI's predictive capabilities are valuable in the realm of blockchain since they can be used for fraud detection and prevention. By analyzing transaction patterns and identifying anomalies, AI systems can flag suspicious activities, providing an additional layer of security. This is yet another way that AI can potentially protect blockchain networks from threats to ensure the integrity of transactions and build trust with users.

Meanwhile, in the realm of investing, predictive analytics can offer insights into market trends and trading strategies, empowering investors with data-driven decisions. This could look like a system that continuously scans market data by using AI to predict price movements and recommend optimal trading strategies. This type of system could level the playing field for all investors. In the area of scalability, AI algorithms could be used to optimize data processing and resource allocation, which would increase the number of transactions that a blockchain network can handle. In other words, AI could be used to help solve one of crypto's biggest problems!

Together, AI and the blockchain hold the potential to offer more secure and private solutions for users. The blockchain's decentralized structure ensures data is distributed across numerous nodes, reducing the risk of centralized breaches. AI holds the ability to encrypt and analyze data, allowing robust protection for sensitive information. However, despite these promising advancements, integrating AI and the blockchain presents challenges.

First, AI models are prone to bias. To avoid this bias, they must be trained on diverse and representative data sets that aren't prejudiced—otherwise, these data sets could skew results. Another challenge is security. AI often requires immense data sets that can be security hazards in the event of a hack. Additionally, the regulatory landscape poses challenges because laws for AI and the blockchain are still evolving. The industry will need to keep close tabs on emerging regulations. Getting the regulations right will require close collaboration between industry leaders, policymakers, and technologists to establish standards that balance innovation with consumer protection.

Reflection Section: Exploring AI and Blockchain Integration

Consider the implications of combining AI and blockchain in your field. How could these technologies transform your industry or personal projects? Reflect on potential applications, challenges, and the skills needed to navigate this intersection.

Scaling Solutions: Layer 2 and Beyond

The scalability problem is still a big issue. However, several solutions have already succeeded in making headway. One of the most noteworthy solutions is called Layer 2, and it's set to be a big part of scalability in crypto going forward. Layer 2 solutions work alongside the main blockchain (Layer 1) to make it faster and less crowded without changing its core design.

One prominent example of Layer 2 is the Lightning Network, which works alongside Bitcoin to make transactions faster by packaging them together. The Lightning Network operates by a smart contract that allows users to create channels. When a channel is open, it accepts transactions. Once closed, the channel packages these transactions together and sends them to the Bitcoin blockchain to be officially processed. This reduces the workload on Layer 1, the Bitcoin network. Instead of having to process ten different transactions, for example, Bitcoin can now just process the one packaged transaction (Nevil, 2025). This makes transactions faster, cheaper, and easier for users, improving the overall experience while keeping the system safe.

When multiple transactions are combined like this, it's called a rollup. These bundled transactions are typically processed off-chain, converted into a single piece of data, and then submitted to the parent chain (such as Bitcoin, Ethereum, etc.). There are two types of rollups that you should know about:

1. **ZK Rollups (Zero-Knowledge Rollups)**: These move both computation and storage off-chain. They're capable of bundling over a thousand transactions and producing a "validity proof" while submitting a minimal summary of what they did to the main blockchain.
2. **Optimistic Rollups**: Instead of providing a "validity proof," these assume all transactions are valid by default. This saves a lot of time, but to combat fraud, they then must include a "challenge period" after the batch is submitted to the main blockchain. If someone suspects an error, they can then challenge the batch. When a transaction is proven to be illegitimate, the rollup protocol then re-executes things appropriately and issues a penalty to the block validator.

Optimistic rollups have the advantage of being easier to implement and less expensive compared to ZK rollups (Ledger, 2023).

Both types of rollups significantly improve blockchain scalability by enabling more transactions to be processed per second. They are particularly useful for applications like DeFi, gaming, and NFTs, where high speed and security are critical. They've already made a huge difference on Ethereum by reducing congestion and improving the user experience. As blockchain technology develops, rollups should play a key role in making blockchains ready for mass adoption, supporting a wide range of apps and services without delays or high costs. Eventually, the goal is a future where blockchains can handle millions of users seamlessly.

Alongside Layer 2 solutions, there are Layer 1 solutions that can help to improve scalability. One example is sharding. Ethereum 2.0 already implements sharding, but in the future, it's set to take sharding to a new level with the introduction of technologies like danksharding. We previously talked about sharding and danksharding in the last subsection of chapter two. Sharding is a strategy for increasing scalability by splitting the blockchain into smaller segments that process transactions simultaneously. Danksharding is a new type of sharding that will potentially improve scalability even further.

Beyond sharding, another important step to improve blockchain technology is cross-chain interoperability. This is the concept of creating a connected ecosystem where assets and data can communicate and share information easily and freely between networks. For example, imagine transferring cryptocurrency or using applications from Solana on Ethereum without any barriers or middlemen—this is what interoperability enables.

Currently, many blockchains operate as separate "islands" where assets and applications are locked within their own systems. This lack of connection, known as fragmentation, limits the potential of blockchain technology. Cross-chain interoperability would allow users to access a wider range of services, similar to the way enabling different technological devices to speak with each other unlocked new frontiers. In the past, our laptops were separate from our phones, which were separate from our TVs.

Now, we can seamlessly Airdrop pictures from our phones to our computers or other phones, and we can cast our laptop screens to our TVs without the need for a cord or any fancy tech.

Projects like Polkadot and Cosmos are leading the way in interoperability. These platforms act as "bridges" that connect different blockchains, allowing them to exchange data and assets securely. For instance, Polkadot uses parachains to link multiple blockchains, while Cosmos utilizes a Cosmos Hub to translate the languages of connected blockchains (Cryptodaily.co.uk, 2022).

This interconnectedness not only makes blockchains more efficient; it encourages innovation. In the future, we may see developers combining the unique features of multiple blockchains to build better applications, such as by leveraging one blockchain's speed with another's security. In this way, cross-chain interoperability is paving the way for a more unified and innovative digital world where the full potential of blockchain technology can be realized.

One of the biggest challenges to future scalability is security. With Layer 2 solutions in particular, security can be a big issue because any vulnerability in a Layer 2 solution could compromise the entire network's integrity.

Furthermore, integrating Layer 2 solutions with existing infrastructure can present a significant hurdle. Many users and developers are accustomed to the current blockchain systems, and transitioning to new technologies will require education, adaptation, and trust.

Implementing Layer 2 solutions can be complex, which presents another barrier. To work, any Layer 2 solution needs sufficient liquidity. Without that, trades become nearly impossible. Future technologies will need to address these technical challenges if they hope to achieve widespread adoption and success.

Energy Consumption and Sustainability: Greening Crypto

PoW algorithms can require significant amounts of energy. In Chapter 1, we talked about how the energy required for Bitcoin alone rivals that of entire countries. This energy-intensive process is poised to be a big problem in the future, especially when large swaths of this energy come from non-renewable sources that contribute to the rise of carbon in our atmosphere.

To mitigate the environmental impact, there are a few different solutions the crypto ecosystem may move towards in the future:

- **Proof-of-Stake (PoS):** Unlike PoW, which requires miners to expend computational energy, PoS relies on validators that are chosen based on the number of tokens they hold and are willing to "stake" as collateral. This shift significantly reduces energy consumption because it eliminates the need for intensive computational work. Ethereum has already transitioned to PoS with its Ethereum 2.0 upgrade. However, other networks face big hurdles in transitioning, given how long it's been operating as a PoW network and its history of resisting change in an effort to stay true to Satoshi's vision.
- **Renewable Energy Sources:** By leveraging solar, wind, and hydroelectric power, PoW cryptocurrencies like Bitcoin can reduce

their reliance on fossil fuels, cutting down their carbon emissions and promoting a greener crypto ecosystem. There's also a growing trend called "green mining," where operations use new technologies to reuse energy that would otherwise go to waste.

- **Improved Algorithms:** Some crypto projects are already finding ways to reduce the energy needed for mining by improving algorithms. In the future, this process may accelerate as advancements in speed and efficiency enable mining architecture to operate with less energy.
- **Carbon Offsets:** This is when miners engage in activities like reforestation to cancel out their emissions.

One notable example of industry-led sustainability is the creation of blockchain networks that integrate eco-friendly practices from the ground up. These networks are designed to be energy-efficient through the incorporation of consensus mechanisms that minimize environmental impact. By prioritizing sustainability in their architecture, they aim to set a new standard for blockchain technology, demonstrating that digital innovation can coexist with environmental responsibility.

In the future, regulation will play an important role in promoting sustainable practices in the cryptocurrency industry. Ultimately, it will be up to governments to create rules and offer incentives to encourage greener mining operations while discouraging harmful ones. One idea might be to implement a system of carbon credits. In this system, mining companies that use fossil fuels would need to buy credits, making their operations more expensive. On the other hand, companies that use clean energy such as wind, solar, or hydropower could sell their unused credits, earning money while helping the environment. Another option might be to phase out fossil fuels altogether with strict regulation. As coal, oil, and other energy sources become less available, miners could be required to either pay more for energy or find alternative ways of generating energy. Additionally, governments could set rules requiring mining companies to use renewable energy and offer tax breaks or funding to those meeting environmental standards.

As cryptocurrency continues to evolve, its sustainability will remain a big focal point of discussion and development. The transition to more energy-efficient protocols, the adoption of renewable energy, and the implementation of regulatory measures all represent steps toward a greener crypto ecosystem. While challenges remain, the industry's movement towards sustainability with technologies like Ethereum 2.0 is encouraging, suggesting that it is possible to harness the benefits of blockchain technology without compromising our planet's health.

The Metaverse: Crypto's Role in Virtual Worlds

Imagine a vast, persistent digital universe where you can socialize, work, shop, and play without ever leaving your home. This is the metaverse. In this shared world, the boundaries between the digital and physical blur, offering an experience that might seem like science fiction. Cryptocurrencies are poised to serve as the financial backbone of this metaverse, and in the future, we might expect them to integrate with Augmented Reality (AR) or Virtual Reality (VR) to create more fulfilling and immersive experiences.

Alongside crypto, NFTs may add another layer to the metaverse, providing a mechanism for ownership and verification of unique digital items. Whether it's a piece of virtual real estate, digital art, or an avatar's clothing, NFTs would ensure that ownership is clear and transferable. This system could both support commerce and encourage creativity as users invent and monetize new products and services. Here are some examples of NFTs you might expect to see in the metaverse:

- **Digital Art:** paintings, drawings, or other illustrations
- **In-Game Assets:** weapon skins or accessories
- **Virtual Real Estate:** shops or event spaces

Platforms like Decentraland and Axie Infinity are already breaking ground in the metaverse. Decentraland allows users to buy, develop, and sell virtual real estate. For example, someone might purchase a digital plot of land, build a virtual store or event space, and then sell or rent it for a profit. All transactions are recorded on the blockchain, making ownership transparent and secure, similar to how real-world property deeds work.

Meanwhile, Axie Infinity is a "play-to-earn" game where users breed, train, and battle virtual creatures called Axies. Players earn cryptocurrency through gameplay, such as by winning battles or selling rare Axies in the marketplace. This allows players to both make some money and enjoy an immersive, fun game.

Furthermore, as digital identities become more prevalent, the metaverse might help us deal with questions of privacy and security. In a world where privacy has become a huge concern for many people, blockchain technology offers secure, decentralized systems for ensuring that users maintain their anonymity when they want. In the metaverse, we could eventually have opportunities for remote work and education without the need for learners or workers to expose personal identifying information. In the metaverse, anyone from anywhere can step into a room together and collaborate. This allows participants from diverse backgrounds to come together in a way they might not be able to in the real world.

As the metaverse continues to develop, its integration with cryptocurrencies will likely deepen, shaping the evolution of digital societies. The financial systems underpinning technologies like Decentraland and Axie Infinity offer a glimpse into the future of commerce when decentralized, user-driven economies likely thrive. This should enable a new era of innovation and interaction without boundaries.

Chapter 10
Integrating Crypto into Everyday Life

Back at the start of this book, we talked about how Bitcoin was used to purchase two Papa John's pizzas in 2010. It's come a long way since then, and while nobody knows what the future holds, it's likely that Bitcoin will integrate even more into our society as time goes on, becoming a viable payment method for not just pizza but also groceries, morning coffee, new laptops or smartphones, and even airline tickets.

In fact, this scenario is not a futuristic dream but a present-day reality. Multiple retailers allow consumers to buy products in Bitcoin right now. We talked about Overstock, Newegg, Expedia, and Microsoft back in Chapter 8. These are just some of the many companies that are making strides to welcome the crypto era.

The use cases for crypto don't stop there. In this chapter, we'll talk about a variety of ways cryptocurrency can and already is being used in everyday life. We'll look at long-term wealth-building strategies, crypto community activities, and more. As crypto continues to grow, it's likely to reshape how we perceive and use money in our daily lives.

Everyday Payments: Using Crypto in Daily Transactions

Recently, cryptocurrency debit cards have emerged as a convenient tool to bridge the gap between digital assets and traditional fiat transactions. By using a crypto debit card, you can spend your digital currencies at any location that accepts regular debit cards. These cards automatically convert your cryptocurrency into local currency at the point of sale, simplifying the process and expanding your financial flexibility. Providers like Crypto.com and Coinbase offer such cards, often with rewards like cashback in crypto. This often works much like credit card rewards work, except that you get paid the rewards in crypto, which means that if crypto goes up in price, the value of your rewards can rise as well!

One significant benefit of using crypto is the reduction in foreign transaction fees. Crypto cards already require a conversion from cryptocurrency to your native currency, so if you are traveling abroad, there's usually not much extra work involved. With traditional debit cards, cross-border payments can often be slow and expensive because banks need to deal with exchange rates and fees for sending money. With crypto, you get around all of this.

Another way to pay with crypto is by sending money from your crypto wallet to a retailer directly. This method of payment is still in its infancy—there aren't a lot of retailers that will accept payment in this way. When sending money from your wallet, you'll usually just need the wallet address of the recipient to whom you are sending it. In some cases, you can also use a QR code that the recipient generates to get the wallet address. This makes it a lot easier because you don't have to worry about making a typo and losing the money.

At present, there are challenges and obstacles to using crypto for daily expenses, including:

- The volatility of crypto prices
- Lack of acceptance by many merchants/retailers
- Scalability issues
- Security issues with exchanges and/or smart contracts

In the future, the hope is that these obstacles can be overcome. With technical achievements to address scalability, increased adoption of crypto as an asset, and regulations to keep the crypto market financially secure, we can create a future in which crypto is as easy to use for payment as the internet is to use for research right now.

Crypto Spending Checklist

Here are some tips for using and spending crypto in your daily life:

1. **Research Retailers:** Identify and support businesses that accept crypto payments.
2. **Use Crypto Debit Cards:** Apply for a card to facilitate daily transactions.

3. **Monitor Market Conditions:** Stay informed about price trends to make informed spending decisions.
4. **Set Conversion Alerts:** Use apps to notify you when favorable conversion rates are available.
5. **Diversify Payment Methods:** Combine crypto with traditional payment options for flexibility.

Building a Crypto-Friendly Lifestyle: Tools and Tips

Cultivating a crypto-friendly lifestyle involves more than just using the right tools; it requires aligning your lifestyle choices with the cryptocurrency ethos. One way to do this is by supporting businesses that accept crypto payments, thereby encouraging wider adoption. Engaging with online communities can also enhance your experience, providing opportunities to share insights, discuss trends, and learn from others who are equally passionate about digital currencies. These interactions can help to build community and friendships, as well as encourage individual growth.

A big part of the crypto lifestyle is practicing healthy security habits. You should use hardware wallets for safe storage if you have a significant amount of crypto, and you should make sure to keep the recovery phrases in a safe space that you will remember but that others won't find. Regularly updating your software and conducting security checks on your devices are also important. When these strategies are combined, they ensure that you remain in control of your investments, minimizing the risk of losing any money to malicious actors.

It's also important to balance crypto with traditional financial investments. Consider diversifying your income streams by including crypto investments as only a part of your broader financial strategy. This diversification is a hedge against market fluctuations, whether those come from the crypto market or the stock market. This can allow you to enjoy the benefits of both the crypto and traditional finance markets while minimizing risk.

Long-Term Wealth Strategies: Planning for the Future

As you look to build wealth, incorporate cryptocurrencies into long-term financial planning. The cryptocurrency market is still young, so if you're investing early in life, you have a lot of time to make money as it matures. Keep this in mind as you invest. You could integrate digital assets like Bitcoin or Ethereum into your retirement portfolio through crypto IRAs or Bitcoin ETFs. You could also invest in crypto and put it away in cold storage, which means storing it on a hardware wallet that is disconnected from the internet. By allocating a portion of your savings to crypto, you position yourself to capitalize on the growth potential over the coming decades. Furthermore, if the assets rise in price enough, then it will give you something to leave to your children or other loved ones when you pass.

Historically, digital assets have significantly appreciated over time, rewarding patient investors. This means that adopting a long-term investment approach is likely the safest way to generate earnings. When you invest long-term, it doesn't matter if Bitcoin loses $10,000 worth of value overnight. It only matters how valuable it is five, 10, 15, or 20 years from now.

However, long-term crypto investments do come with some risks and challenges. Regulatory changes can significantly impact the value of the assets. As governments iron out their policies, it's anyone's guess what laws and regulations will look like in the future. Policy shifts could influence market dynamics and investor sentiment. Additionally, technological obsolescence poses a threat. The rapid pace of innovation in the blockchain space means that today's leading cryptocurrency could be overshadowed by tomorrow's technological advancements. Being aware of these risks and adapting to them is crucial for making informed decisions.

To effectively manage and grow your crypto wealth, consider implementing strategic approaches that are tailored to long-term success.

- **Periodic Rebalancing of Your Cryptocurrency Portfolio:** This is to make sure that your asset allocation aligns with your financial goals and risk tolerance. By regularly reviewing and adjusting your holdings, you can optimize for growth while mitigating risks.

- **Leveraging Tax-Advantaged Accounts:** Some jurisdictions offer accounts that provide tax benefits for investments, including cryptocurrencies. For example, in the United States, self-directed IRAs and Solo 401(k)s can be used to hold cryptocurrency investments while enjoying tax-deferred or tax-free growth. Similarly, in Canada, a Tax-Free Savings Account (TFSA) allows individuals to invest in crypto without paying taxes on the gains.

By taking advantage of these opportunities, you can grow your returns while minimizing tax liabilities. Just be aware that some of these solutions, such as buying crypto through a Crypto IRA, come with the same risks as investing your money via a crypto exchange. These are centralized services, which means that if the company goes under, you might not be protected.

Education and Community: Engaging with Crypto Networks

For those of us who engage with the crypto community, staying educated is important. Technology is rapidly evolving, and demands are changing, which means that we need to stay informed and adaptable.

Online courses and webinars are two great ways to deepen your understanding of the crypto space. These courses often offer structured learning experiences for you to explore complex topics at your own pace. Alongside these courses, reading reputable crypto research articles and newsletters, as well as listening to podcasts, can further enrich your knowledge with insights into market trends, technological advancements, and regulatory developments.

Staying informed is not just about keeping up with the latest news; it's about understanding the underlying principles that drive the crypto market. Here are a few resources that you can use to better understand these principles:

- **Explain Bitcoin Like I'm Five:** A simple primer by angel investor Nik Custodio

- **But How Does Bitcoin Actually Work?:** A YouTube explainer video by the channel 3Blue1Brown
- **Bitcoin Whitepaper:** Satoshi's original whitepaper, published shortly before Bitcoin went live
- **Ethereum in 25 Minutes:** A YouTube talk where Vitalik Buterin, the co-founder of Ethereum, explains how it works
- **Ethereum Whitepaper:** The whitepaper detailing the ins and outs of Ethereum
- **10 Important Cryptocurrencies Other Than Bitcoin:** A guide put out by Investopedia about some of the most popular altcoins
- **A Beginner's Guide to Decentralized Finance (DeFi):** A Coinbase blog post that goes through the intricacies of DeFi
- **Bankless:** A crypto podcast and newsletter
- **Unchained:** A crypto podcast and news website (Coinbase, n.d.-a)

In addition to staying informed, keeping up with the crypto community is a big part of education. By joining forums and discussion groups, you can exchange ideas and insights with other enthusiasts and experts. These platforms can serve as vibrant hubs for sharing experiences, discussing trends, and troubleshooting challenges. You can also increase your understanding by attending crypto meetups and conferences to find mentorship and collaboration in the crypto space.

Here are some of the ways you can engage with the crypto community online:

- **Telegram:** This is a messaging app that also offers groups for likeminded individuals to get together and chat. Telegram has several crypto communities, such as the Bitget Official Telegram Community.
- **Discord:** Like Telegram, Discord offers communities that you can join to chat with likeminded people. You can find channels related to NFTs, DeFi, technical analysis, and more.
- **X (formerly Twitter):** You can engage with the community by following influencers in the space, such as Vitalik Buterin, or following projects or crypto analysts.
- **Reddit Subreddits:** You can engage with people who have niche interests in the

crypto space or with larger groups of people in subreddits like r/CryptoCurrency and r/Bitcoin. There's a subreddit for almost anything.

- **Online Forums**: You might find communities on websites specializing in crypto, like Bitcointalk or CryptoCompare, or you might find them on more mainstream sites like Quora (Basiru, 2024).

Finding a mentor with experience and expertise in your community can be a big help. A mentor's invaluable insights help you avoid common pitfalls and capitalize on emerging opportunities. Additionally, a mentor can help you to get involved in collaborative projects and initiatives that further enhance your experience. This collaborative spirit fosters innovation and creativity, amplifying your impact and expanding your horizons. Contributing to open-source crypto projects is a particularly powerful way to get involved with the community while gaining practical experience. These projects offer opportunities to collaborate with others, develop new skills, and contribute to the advancement of the crypto ecosystem.

Ultimately, by prioritizing continuous learning, engaging with communities, and collaborating with others, you can position yourself to thrive in the ever-evolving field of digital finance. As you navigate the crypto world in the future, remember that education and community are what this is all about. Nobody succeeds alone.

Addressing Volatility: Thriving in a Dynamic Market

Dealing with market volatility doesn't just involve executing the right strategies to mitigate its effect on your finances. It also involves addressing the emotional challenges that volatility poses. It's not easy to watch your investments fluctuate wildly in price without doing anything. Maintaining a long-term perspective is the most important part of dealing with volatility because it helps you focus on your broader financial goals rather than short-term market trends.

Emotional resilience is key to making it through the rough times without succumbing to fear or impulsivity. To become more emotionally resilient and disciplined, you might consider reading books about critical thinking or overthinking. Such resources can provide valuable insights about managing emotions; that way, you can improve your decision-making and keep a cool head. By cultivating this mindset, you can more easily weather the storms of volatility in the market.

Additionally, volatility indicators, such as Crypto's Fear and Greed Index, which we discussed earlier, can be a big help. Engaging with a professional financial advisor offers you expertise and an external perspective to guide you through complex market conditions. Advisors can assist in tailoring strategies that align with your financial objectives and risk tolerance to ensure you remain on track despite market fluctuations. Another tactic is to start small, especially if you find yourself learning crypto investing on your own and going it alone. When you start small, you give yourself a chance to learn crypto first, which lessens the chance of you losing any significant amount of money.

Continuous Learning: Staying Informed and Adaptable

Stay informed to keep up with the new technologies and regulations that are emerging in crypto. Following thought leaders and experts in the field can be a great way to remain abreast of market trends and technological advancements. These individuals often share their knowledge through blogs, social media, and speaking engagements, offering a wealth of information to help you stay ahead. Subscribing to cryptocurrency newsletters and podcasts is another effective way to stay updated. Bankless and Unchained, the two resources we discussed earlier, are great resources.

Adaptability in crypto investing is equally important. Be open to new technologies and explore innovative solutions to capitalize on emerging opportunities. For instance, when Solana first came out, there were several cryptocurrencies similar to it, including Ethereum, which was and remains the second-largest crypto by market cap. However, Solana quickly carved out a spot in the crypto ecosystem with its improved scalability, and smart investors adapted quickly, incorporating it into their portfolios. Staying attuned to market shifts like this will enable you to refine your approach and make the most of your money.

To maintain a learning mindset, consider setting aside dedicated time for regular study sessions as part of your daily routine. This commitment can and will enable you to make better-informed decisions. Similarly, engaging in peer learning and knowledge sharing can further enhance your understanding. If you learn something useful, don't be afraid to share it with your online community. If they share something, be sure to pay attention. While you share and discuss ideas, explore different viewpoints, and expand your perspective in collaborative environments where you can learn from others' experiences and insights, enriching your knowledge and broadening your horizons.

By staying informed, remaining open to change, and fostering a learning mindset, you can become more confident, leading to better investment decisions and more awareness about how cryptocurrency is influencing the world. Remember, this isn't just about preparing you for the future. It's also about creating an environment and a community that makes the world a better place.

Afterword

Cryptocurrency isn't just money that's on a computer. It's my hope that by now, you can see why it's so much more than that. The "crypto" part of cryptocurrency comes from the fact that your money is kept secure through cryptographic means. To handle this cryptography, Bitcoin revolutionized digital currencies by introducing a new technology called the blockchain. With the blockchain, computers all over the world store information about who owns what amount of Bitcoin. No new transactions can be approved unless a majority of those computers—over 51 percent—agree that the transaction is valid.

Since the inventor of Bitcoin, Satoshi Nakamoto, published their whitepaper and unleashed blockchain technology upon the world, an enormous number of cryptocurrencies have come into the public sphere. Ethereum gained recognition for introducing smart contracts. Solana improved on transaction speeds. And many cryptocurrencies transitioned from Proof of Work to Proof of Stake, lowering the energy required to keep the network running by an astronomical amount.

Amid all this, decentralization and transparency have remained core tenets of how crypto works. There are centralized technologies that work with the crypto ecosystem, but all the leaders in the space and the most impactful crypto is decentralized. As we've seen, there's a good reason for this. Centralized exchanges have been where almost all frauds and hacks have taken place. From Mt. Gox back in 2014 to the recent implosion of FTX, there are many reasons why decentralization is the future.

As you go forth and invest, keep in mind some of the risk-management strategies we have discussed. Making money in crypto isn't easy; it's not going to happen overnight. Start small so you can learn the ropes. Look at reputable sources to learn about different coins before you buy them. Be careful about where you buy crypto—there are a lot of shady people out there who may take advantage of those who don't understand the space yet. Go to reputable exchanges like Coinbase and Binance, or buy through a reputable wallet like Ledger. They have guides that will walk you through purchasing crypto. And be careful of ICOs! You don't want to fall into a pump-and-dump scheme.

When you integrate into the crypto community, you will have the power to shape the future of crypto. These digital currencies can be a force for good, improving the world rather than harming it, but we must make it so. Do your best to support technologies that democratize access to finance, lower fees for the everyday user, reduce the energy consumption of crypto networks, and keep people's funds secure from hackers and thieves.

Also, don't forget to stay up to date on how crypto is integrating with existing systems. Many industries are already beginning to use blockchain technology to improve the way they do things. Meanwhile, banks have crafted their own centralized cryptocurrencies, and some countries are doing the same with CBDCs. There's no telling how all of these changes could affect the future, but by staying up to date, you can use the information to make smarter investments and to stay prepared, whether that means coexisting with a digital space, interacting with AI to access the blockchain, or spending money directly from digital wallets on our phones.

Keep these three things in mind as you go out into the world:

1. **Always Be Learning:** Whether that means taking a course, reading a book, listening to a podcast, reading news articles, or talking with the crypto community, learning is a core part of how you will keep up with all the changes. Crypto is a dynamic world. Just 10 years ago, there was no Ethereum and no smart contracts. Five years ago, Ethereum was still running as a PoW network instead of PoS. Two years ago, there were no Bitcoin ETFs. These are just some of the changes that have come about recently. Between the time I've written this book and the time you read it, there will probably be even more changes in the crypto world—maybe some huge ones! You'll only know about them if

you keep learning and adding to your knowledge.

2. **Don't Fall for the Hype, but Stay Adaptable:** It's easy to get caught up in the emotions of trading crypto. This is a big reason why a lot of people invest using DCA method, putting in a little bit every week or month. However, there is also some power in staying adaptable. Do your best to make clearheaded decisions. If a new cryptocurrency comes out that looks promising, do your research, and then if things check out, invest in a thoughtful way. If, on the other hand, news comes out that affects a cryptocurrency's underlying technology, don't be afraid to rebalance your portfolio away from that piece of crypto.
3. **Diversify:** Just because a cryptocurrency existed first doesn't mean it will succeed above others. Bitcoin and Ethereum are currently two of the biggest cryptocurrencies, but plenty of other crypto is worth holding as well. And while Bitcoin was the first cryptocurrency, Ethereum was definitely not the second one. Plenty of others emerged between 2009 and 2015

> when Ethereum came out, such as Litecoin. Diversifying is a good idea in almost any area of life. There's even a saying that goes, "Don't put all your eggs in one basket." Don't put all your crypto on one network, either. This is especially true for exchanges. Remember, that's where almost all the hacks and thefts occur. You might diversify by splitting your money across exchanges and hardware wallets or investing your money through multiple different exchanges.

So, go ahead and get started. Before you buy any crypto, look at some of the communities out there and join one or two. Respond to posts in Reddit forums or chat with others on social media who are talking about Bitcoin, Ethereum, or any other crypto that catches your eye. Start with large communities, because these are the places you're most likely to easily meet people who are trustworthy. In smaller communities, it's easier for fraudsters to fly under the radar. These communities can be less active and may even be run by people with malicious intentions. If you join a large subreddit, for instance, you can be sure that the people there are looking to engage with others in discussing crypto. If they weren't, the group wouldn't be so successful.

Good luck, and thank you for reading! I sincerely hope you've learned everything you set out to from this book. I welcome your feedback and insights. If I missed anything or got something wrong, please let me know. I'm only human. With anything in the decentralized crypto ecosystem, the power of this knowledge comes from how the community engages with it. We must all build a decentralized future, working together to make the world a better place. Like the many nodes in a blockchain network, no one person can create this change. The change comes from our shared agreement on a better future and better technology. This is the power of decentralization.

Before we part ways, I have one quick favor to ask. Cryptocurrency is still misunderstood by many—often judged by hype, fear, or noise from people who haven't taken the time to really learn how it works.

If this book helped shift your thinking or gave you something valuable to consider, I'd be grateful if you shared your thoughts on Amazon or Goodreads. Your honest opinion might encourage someone else to take their first step toward financial clarity and confidence.

I'd also love to know how you're thinking about crypto now—and what questions or ideas you're exploring next.

If you're interested in going deeper, I regularly share **bonus content, exclusive insights, and early previews** through my BookFunnel VIP page. It's a space for readers who want to stay ahead of the curve—quietly and confidently.

Visit: https://dl.bookfunnel.com/w30ai1rzn6

You're warmly invited to join the list and get first access to special material I don't share anywhere else.

The future of money is already here. Let's make sure you're not just watching from the sidelines—but navigating it with clarity.

Warmly,

Troy Brexton

Glossary

51 Percent Attack: A network vulnerability in which a group controlling the majority of computing power manipulates blockchain transactions.

Airdrop: A marketing strategy in which free cryptocurrency tokens are distributed to wallet addresses to promote a project.

Altcoin: Any cryptocurrency other than Bitcoin, such as Ethereum, Litecoin, or Ripple, offering unique features or improvements over Bitcoin.

Altseason: A period when altcoins (non-Bitcoin cryptocurrencies) experience significant price increases compared to Bitcoin.

Atomic Swap: A smart contract technology enabling the direct exchange of cryptocurrencies between two parties without intermediaries.

Bitcoin (BTC): The first cryptocurrency, created in 2009 by Satoshi Nakamoto, was designed as a decentralized digital alternative to traditional currencies.

Block: A structure storing transaction data on the blockchain, linked to previous blocks to form a chain.

Blockchain: A decentralized digital ledger that records transactions across a network, ensuring transparency and security by storing data in sequentially linked blocks.

Blockchain Explorer: A tool that allows users to search and view detailed blockchain transaction histories, wallet balances, and other on-chain data.

Burning: The process of permanently removing cryptocurrency from circulation, reducing supply to increase value.

Centralized Exchange (CEX): A cryptocurrency exchange managed by a central authority, such as Binance or Coinbase, offering user-friendly services.

Cold Wallet: A cryptocurrency wallet not connected to the internet, offering enhanced security for storing digital assets offline.

Consensus Attack: An attack that disrupts the consensus mechanism, such as Sybil attacks or Byzantine Fault Tolerance exploits.

Consensus Mechanism: The method by which blockchain networks agree on the validity of transactions, such as Proof of Work or Proof of Stake.

Cross-Chain: The ability to transfer data or tokens between different blockchain networks, enabling interoperability.

Cryptocurrency: A digital currency secured by cryptography, operating on blockchain technology, which enables secure and decentralized transactions.

DApp (Decentralized Application): Applications built on a blockchain that run autonomously without a central authority, enhancing security and transparency.

DeFi (Decentralized Finance): Blockchain-based financial services that eliminate intermediaries and offer lending, borrowing, and trading directly between users.

Decentralization: The distribution of control across a network, eliminating the need for central authorities like banks or governments.

Decentralized Exchange (DEX): A peer-to-peer platform allowing users to trade cryptocurrencies directly without intermediaries, like Uniswap or PancakeSwap.

Double Spending: A potential issue caused when the same cryptocurrency unit is spent more than once, prevented by blockchain's consensus mechanisms.

Dusting Attack: A malicious tactic in which attackers send tiny amounts of cryptocurrency to wallets to de-anonymize users.

Ethereum (ETH): A blockchain platform enabling smart contracts and decentralized applications, with Ether as its native cryptocurrency.

Fiat Currency: Traditional government-issued currency like the U.S. Dollar (USD) or Euro (EUR); often used to trade cryptocurrencies.

Fork: A change in blockchain protocol rules, resulting in a network split or the creation of a new blockchain version.

Gas Fees: Transaction fees paid to blockchain miners or validators for processing and securing network transactions.

Gas Limit: The maximum amount of computational effort a user is willing to pay for when executing a blockchain transaction.

Halving: A programmed event in some cryptocurrencies that reduces mining rewards by half approximately every four years to control supply.

Hash: A unique string of characters generated by algorithms to represent data securely on the blockchain.

Hash Rate: The total computational power used in mining or validating transactions on a blockchain network.

HODL: A slang term meaning "Hold On for Dear Life," encouraging long-term holding of cryptocurrency despite market volatility.

Hot Wallet: A cryptocurrency wallet connected to the internet, providing convenient access but with higher security risks compared to cold wallets.

ICO (Initial Coin Offering): A fundraising method in which new cryptocurrencies or tokens are sold to investors to fund blockchain projects.

Immutable: A key blockchain feature; data, once written, cannot be altered or deleted, ensuring trust and transparency.

Initial Exchange Offering (IEO): A fundraising event by a cryptocurrency project that sells its tokens through a centralized exchange.

Layer 2 Solution: Secondary frameworks or protocols, like Lightning Network, that are built on top of blockchains to improve scalability and transaction speed.

Ledger: A record-keeping system used to track cryptocurrency transactions securely and transparently across a blockchain.

Liquidity: The ability to quickly convert an asset, like cryptocurrency, into cash or another cryptocurrency without significantly affecting its price.

Liquidity Pool: A collection of funds locked in a smart contract to facilitate trading on decentralized exchanges.

Market Cap (Market Capitalization): The total value of a cryptocurrency, calculated by multiplying its current price by the total number of coins in circulation.

Merkle Tree: A cryptographic structure used in blockchain to efficiently organize and verify large sets of transaction data.

Mining: The process of verifying blockchain transactions and adding them to the ledger, often involving computational tasks.

NFT (Non-Fungible Token): A unique digital asset representing ownership of a specific item on a blockchain.

Node: A computer in a blockchain network that stores, verifies, and shares a complete copy of the blockchain ledger.

Oracle: A service or protocol that connects blockchains to external data sources, enabling smart contracts to interact with real-world information.

Paper Wallet: A physical document containing your cryptocurrency private and public keys for offline security.

P2P (Peer-to-Peer): A decentralized interaction system enabling users to transact directly without intermediaries or central control.

Private Key: A confidential code granting access to your cryptocurrency funds; essential for signing transactions.

Proof of Stake (PoS): A consensus method that selects validators based on the number of coins they stake in the network.

Proof of Work (PoW): A consensus mechanism requiring miners to solve mathematical problems to validate blockchain transactions.

Public Key: A cryptographic address shared with others to receive cryptocurrency payments securely.

Rug Pull: A type of scam in DeFi in which developers abandon a project and take investors' funds. This is essentially the same as pump-and-dump.

Satoshi: The smallest unit of Bitcoin, equal to

0.00000001 BTC, named after its creator, Satoshi Nakamoto.

Seed Phrase: A series of words used to back up and recover access to a cryptocurrency wallet in case of loss.

Smart Contract: Self-executing code on a blockchain that enforces agreements without intermediaries, ensuring automated and transparent transactions.

Smart Contract Audit: A review of a smart contract's code to identify vulnerabilities and ensure security.

Stablecoin: A cryptocurrency pegged to stable assets like fiat currency (e.g., USD), reducing price volatility in digital transactions.

Staking: The process of locking up cryptocurrency to support a blockchain network, earning rewards in return.

Token: A digital asset issued on a blockchain that represents value, utility, or ownership, often used within specific platforms.

Tokenomics: The study of a token's economic

model, including supply, demand, utility, and distribution mechanisms.

Wallet: A digital tool for securely storing, sending, and receiving cryptocurrencies, available as hardware or software applications.

Whale: An individual or entity holding a large amount of cryptocurrency and capable of influencing market prices.

Yield Farming: A DeFi practice in which users provide liquidity to earn rewards, typically in the form of tokens or interest.

Zero-Knowledge Proof: A cryptographic method allowing one party to prove they know something without revealing the actual information.

Bibliography

Akudo. (2023, January 27). *DAOs, dApps & DeFi for dummies*. Medium. https://medium.com/@akudo.in/daos-dapps-defi-for-dummies-2dfb14897021

Amure, T. O. (2024, August 31). *What charts should crypto investors use?* Investopedia. https://www.investopedia.com/charts-for-crypto-6500665

Associated Press. (2023, January 13). *Miami Heat home arena gets temporary name after FTX collapse*. NBA.Com. https://www.nba.com/news/miami-heat-home-arena-gets-temporary-name-after-ftx-collapse

Barr, K. (2022, November 15). *Vast majority of people who invest in Bitcoin inevitably lose money, study shows*. Gizmodo. https://gizmodo.com/bitcoin-crypto-bank-of-international-settlements-1849784466

Basiru, A. (2024). *What are the best communities where I can talk with others about crypto?* Quora. https://www.quora.com/What-are-the-best-communities-where-I-can-talk-with-others-about-crypto

Bertch, R. (2024, November 1). *How cryptocurrency is helping the globe's unbanked*. Fremont Tribune. https://fremonttribune.com/life-entertainment/how-cryptocurrency-is-helping-the-globe-s-unbanked/article_136ead33-8e15-5a02-b8bd-1371460243bd.html

Browne, E. (2021, April 21). *Dogecoin investor becomes millionaire after putting life savings into token*. Newsweek. https://www.newsweek.com/dogecoin-millionaire-investor-life-savings-crypto-meme-1584183

Chaturvedi, V. (2025, January 7). *The history of Bitcoin*. Yahoo

Finance. https://finance.yahoo.com/news/history-bitcoin-151000157.html

Chen, J. (2022, April 6). *What is a contrarian? Strategy in trading, risks, and rewards.* Investopedia. https://www.investopedia.com/terms/c/contrarian.asp

Chen, J. (2024a, June 19). *Double Top and Bottom patterns defined, plus how to use them.* Investopedia. https://www.investopedia.com/terms/d/double-top-and-bottom.asp

Chen, M. (2024b, August 8). *Revolutionizing logistics: How blockchain is transforming supply chains.* Oracle. https://www.oracle.com/blockchain/what-is-blockchain/blockchain-for-supply-chain/

Coinbase. (n.d.-a). *Crypto resources: What to read, watch, and stream in crypto.* https://www.coinbase.com/learn/crypto-basics/essential-reading

Coinbase. (n.d.-b). *Utility tokens vs. security tokens: What are the differences?* https://www.coinbase.com/learn/crypto-basics/utility-tokens-vs-security-tokens-what-are-the-differences

Coinbase. (n.d.-c). *What is Bitcoin pizza?* https://www.coinbase.com/learn/crypto-glossary/what-is-bitcoin-pizza

Crawford, L. (2023, September 2). *Uniswap labs announces bug bounty program with rewards up to 2. 25 million usdc.* Blockchain News. https://blockchain.news/news/uniswap-labs-announces-bug-bounty-program-with-rewards-up-to-225-million-usdc

Crypto 101. (2022, August 17). *What is block size?* Bitstamp Learn. https://www.bitstamp.net/learn/crypto-101/what-is-block-size/

Cryptodaily.co.uk. (2022, April 4). *Top 4 leading projects exploring blockchain interoperability.* Crypto News. https://cryptonews.net/news/blockchain/4601655/

Cryptopedia Staff. (2025, February 26). *The DAO: What was the DAO hack?* Gemini. https://www.gemini.com/cryptopedia/the-dao-hack-makerdao

da Silva, J. (2024, December 16). *Bitcoin hits new record high of more* *than $106,000*. BBC. https://www.bbc.com/news/articles/c5yw poloxrxo

Daly, L. (2025, January 23). *Uses for Blockchain in the financial services industry*. The Motley Fool. https://www.fool.com/invest ing/stock-market/market-sectors/financials/blockchain-stocks/ blockchain-in-finance/

Dedezade, E. (2021, April 2). *Here are the biggest celebrities who have launched NFTs*. Decrypt. https://decrypt.co/63694/biggest-celebrities-who-launched-nfts-snoop-dogg-lohan-hirst-grimes

Edwards, P. (2015, February 9). *7 world-changing inventions people thought were dumb fads*. Vox. https://www.vox.com/2015/2/9/ 8004661/fads-inventions-changed-world

Fernando, J. (2024a, August 6). *Moving average (MA): Purpose, uses, formula, and examples*. Investopedia. https://www.investopedia. com/terms/m/movingaverage.asp

Fernando, J. (2024b, November 19). *Relative strength index (RSI) indicator explained with formula*. Investopedia. https://www. investopedia.com/terms/r/rsi.asp

Flipex. (n.d.). *5 (Five) biggest crypto scams of all time*. Retrieved February 25, 2025, from https://www.flipexapp.com/blog/5-five-biggest-crypto-scams-of-all-time

Garnett, A. G. (2025, February 25). *Cryptocurrency scams: 8 crypto cons to avoid*. Britannica Money. https://www.britannica.com/ money/cryptocurrency-scams

Gov, Y. (2024, August 2). *Crypto technical analysis: Head and shoulders pattern, triangles and wedges*. CryptoPotato. https://cryp topotato.com/crypto-technical-analysis-head-and-shoulders-pattern-triangles-and-wedges/

Hayes, A. (2024, September 16). *Blockchain facts: What is it, how it works, and how it can be used*. Investopedia. https://www.investo pedia.com/terms/b/blockchain.asp

Kaur, G. (2023, September 14). *An overview of the cryptocurrency regulations in Asia*. Cointelegraph. https://cointelegraph.com/learn/articles/an-overview-of-the-cryptocurrency-regulations-in-asia

Kolakowski, M. (2021, September 7). *El Salvador accepts Bitcoin as legal tender*. Investopedia. https://www.investopedia.com/el-salvador-accepts-bitcoin-as-legal-tender-5200470

Kumar, R. (2025, January 6). *South Korea's Jeju Island uses NFT cards to promote tourism*. The Crypto Times. https://www.cryptotimes.io/2025/01/06/south-koreas-jeju-island-uses-nft-cards-to-promote-tourism/

Ledger. (2023, May 29). *What are blockchain rollups?* Ledger Academy. https://www.ledger.com/academy/what-are-blockchain-rollups

Ledger Academy. (2024, May 29). *Crypto nodes: What are they and how do they work?* https://www.ledger.com/academy/what-is-a-node-and-why-should-i-operate-one

Ledger Insights. (2024, May 30). *JP Morgan says JPM Coin transactions have "exploded" because of programmability*. https://www.ledgerinsights.com/jp-morgan-says-jpm-coin-transactions-have-exploded-because-of-programmability/

Liebkind, J. (2020, March 22). *How blockchain technology is changing real estate*. Investopedia. https://www.investopedia.com/news/how-blockchain-technology-changing-real-estate/

McDowell, M., & Schulz, M. (2023, January 17). *Digital fashion startup Syky raises $9 million and launches first NFT*. Vogue Business. https://www.voguebusiness.com/technology/digital-fashion-startup-syky-raises-dollar9-million-and-launches-first-nft

Meiterman, C. (2025, January 2). *12 celebrities who have invested in Bitcoin*. UTB. https://usethebitcoin.com/resources/12-celebrities-who-have-invested-in-bitcoin/

Mitchelhill, T. (2023, September 15). *Ethereum Merge anniversary—99% energy drop but centralization fears linger*. CoinTelegraph.

https://cointelegraph.com/news/ethereum-merge-a-year-later-energy-consumption-down-centralization-fears-ongoing

Mohamed, T. (2022, November 14). *Warren Buffett dismissed Bitcoin as a worthless delusion and "rat poison squared." Here are his 16 best quotes about crypto.* Markets Insider. https://markets.businessinsider.com/currencies/news/warren-buffett-best-quotes-bitcoin-cryptocurrencies-investing-rat-poison-squared-2021-1-1029974898

Nambiampurath, R. (2024, May 27). *What was Ethereum 2.0?* Investopedia. https://www.investopedia.com/ethereum-2-0-6455959

Nevil, S. (2024, August 25). *What is markets in crypto-assets (MICA)?* Investopedia. https://www.investopedia.com/what-is-market-in-crypto-assets-6751039

Nevil, S. (2025, February 24). *Layer 1 vs. Layer 2: The difference between blockchain scaling solutions*. Investopedia. https://www.investopedia.com/what-are-layer-1-and-layer-2-blockchain-scaling-solutions-7104877

Office of Public Affairs. (2024, March 28). *Samuel Bankman-Fried sentenced to 25 years for his orchestration of multiple fraudulent schemes*. U.S. Department of Justice. https://www.justice.gov/archives/opa/pr/samuel-bankman-fried-sentenced-25-years-his-orchestration-multiple-fraudulent-schemes

OneSafe Content Team. (2024, December 28). *Citibank wire transfer fees vs crypto transaction costs: What's your move?* OneSafe. https://www.onesafe.io/blog/crypto-vs-citibank-wire-transfer-fees

Pacheco, R. (2024, March 7). *35 companies that accept Bitcoin & crypto as payment in 2024*. Swiss Money. https://swissmoney.com/who-accepts-bitcoin-as-payment

Picardo, E. (2024, September 25). *What is Solana (SOL) and how does SOL crypto work?* Investopedia. https://www.investopedia.com/solana-5210472

Rapal, H. (2024, June 5). *Smart contracts in insurance: Automating claims and payouts*. Legitt Blog: CLM, Electronic Signature & Smart Contract News. https://legittai.com/blog/smart-contracts-in-insurance

Redman, J. (2024, October 18). *Before Bitcoin: 4 early digital currencies and why they collapsed*. Bitcoin News. https://news.bitcoin.com/before-bitcoin-4-early-digital-currencies-and-why-they-collapsed/

Reiff, N. (2024, March 24). *All about the Bitcoin Cash hard fork*. Investopedia. https://www.investopedia.com/news/all-about-bitcoin-cash-hard-fork/

Reiff, N. (2025, January 19). *How healthcare is applying blockchain technology*. Investopedia. https://www.investopedia.com/tech/how-health-care-moving-toward-blockchain/

Rendon, M. (2021). *How open and public cryptocurrencies can help Venezuelans*. https://www.csis.org/analysis/how-open-and-public-cryptocurrencies-can-help-venezuelans

Reuters. (2025, February 3). *Bitcoin drops to 3-week low as Trump tariffs rattle markets*. https://www.reuters.com/markets/currencies/bitcoin-slides-below-100000-tariffs-rattle-markets-2025-02-02/

Rossow, A. (2018, July 24). *How can we make intellectual property rights "smarter" with the blockchain?* Forbes. https://www.forbes.com/sites/andrewrossow/2018/07/24/how-can-we-make-intellectual-property-rights-smarter-with-the-blockchain/

Russell, K. (2013, November 4). *11 hilariously wrong predictions about the internet*. Business Insider. https://www.businessinsider.com/11-hilariously-wrong-internet-predictions-2013-11

Santander UK. (2018, April 12). *Santander launches the first blockchain-based international money transfer service across four countries*. https://www.santander.co.uk/about-santander/media-centre/press-releases/santander-launches-the-first-blockchain-based-international-money-transfer-service-across-four

Schiller, B. (2018, February 5). *On this blockchain-based version of Airbnb, there's no middleman*. Fast Company. https://www.fastcompany.com/40524021/on-this-blockchain-based-version-of-airbnb-theres-no-middleman

Schwartz, B. (2023, October 20). *Sam Bankman-Fried, FTX allies secretly poured $50 million into "dark money" groups, evidence shows*. CNBC. https://www.cnbc.com/2023/10/20/sam-bankman-fried-ftx-allies-donated-millions-in-dark-money.html

Sharma, S. (2024, September 20). *The role of smart contracts in NFT gaming asset trading*. SDLC Corp. https://sdlccorp.com/post/the-role-of-smart-contracts-in-nft-gaming-asset-trading/

Somebody from Breet. (n.d.). *5 biggest crypto scams of all time*. Breet. Retrieved February 25, 2025, from https://breetapp.com/blog/5-biggest-crypto-scams-of-all-time

Stanford Online. (n.d.). *Popular blockchain use cases across industries*. https://online.stanford.edu/popular-blockchain-use-cases-across-industries

Swan Bitcoin. (n.d.). *Next Bitcoin halving: March 26th, 2028 history and what to know!* Retrieved February 24, 2025, from https://www.swanbitcoin.com/education/bitcoin-halving-dates/

The Editors of Encyclopaedia Britannica. (2025, February 25). *Cryptocurrency*. Britannica Money. https://www.britannica.com/money/cryptocurrency

The Investopedia Team. (2024a, June 12). *What are smart contracts on the blockchain and how do they work?* Investopedia. https://www.investopedia.com/terms/s/smart-contracts.asp

The Investopedia Team. (2024b, August 17). *Golden Cross vs. Death Cross: What's the difference?* Investopedia. https://www.investopedia.com/ask/answers/121114/what-difference-between-golden-cross-and-death-cross-pattern.asp

Thompsett, L. (2024, June 12). *Top 10 use cases for blockchain*. FinTech Magazine. https://fintechmagazine.com/articles/top-10-use-cases-for-blockchain

Thompson, C. (2024, April 16). *Bollinger Bands: What they are, and what they tell investors*. Investopedia. https://www.investopedia.com/terms/b/bollingerbands.asp

UNU. (2023, October 24). *UN study reveals the hidden environmental impacts of Bitcoin: Carbon is not the only harmful by-product*. United Nations University. https://unu.edu/press-release/un-study-reveals-hidden-environmental-impacts-bitcoin-carbon-not-only-harmful-product

Wright, T. (2023, October 12). *Changpeng Zhao's tweet 'contributed' to collapse of FTX, claims Caroline Ellison*. CoinTelegraph. https://cointelegraph.com/news/changpeng-zhao-tweet-ftx-collapse-caroline-ellison

Yaffe-Bellany, D. (2024, January 10). *Regulators approve new type of Bitcoin fund, in boon for crypto industry*. New York Times. https://www.nytimes.com/2024/01/10/technology/sec-bitcoin-approval-exchange-traded-funds.html

Young, M., & Baird, K. (2022, May 2). *Ethereum gas fees spike to new highs on latest NFT hype*. BeInCrypto. https://beincrypto.com/ethereum-gas-fees-spike-highs-latest-nft-hype/

Made in the USA
Monee, IL
04 November 2026

67384741R00134